CW00402232

SUPERPLONK SUMMER EDITION 1999

'With his corking reviews and flair for quips,
His nose has launched a thousand sips.'

(Ann Smallman's winning entry in the
Superplonk 99 competition)

'Essential for a summer of pleasurable drinking at an affordable price'

Daily Express

'A splendid volume and very useful for the summer party planner. Best of all are Gluck's unpretentious descriptions and useful rating code'

Wiltshire Times

'An impressive and accessible guide to what's really worth drinking'

Observer

'Gluck has a distinctively brash style which some love and others hate: his descriptive vocabulary is all his own, and some of his judgements turn convention on its head'

Time Out

'The Nick Hornby of the wine world'

Birmingham Post

About the Author

Malcolm Gluck is the *Guardian*'s wine correspondent, writing a regular Saturday column, *Superplonk*. He writes three wine guides a year, each one fresh and fruity and unadulterated by anything but his own singular viewpoint. He presented his own BBC-TV wine series – *Gluck, Gluck, Gluck*. He is consultant wine editor to Sainsbury's Magazine, contributing a monthly wine diary. He has compiled a double-CD of classical music with wine for Deutsche Grammophon. His guide to wine tasting, *The Sensational Liquid*, will be published later this year. Other major preoccupations are his children, dead authors, all styles of piano music, and relaxing in cemeteries.

Superplonk Summer Edition 1999

Malcolm Gluck

coronet

CORONET BOOKS

Hodder & Stoughton

ISBN 0 340 69489 0

Typeset by Palimpsest Book Production Limited,
Polmont, Stirlingshire
Printed and bound in Great Britain by
Clays Ltd, St Ives plc, Bungay, Suffolk

Hodder and Stoughton
A division of Hodder Headline PLC
338 Euston Road
London NW1 3BH

For P.L. – whose books are an inspiration

'The only preface of a work is the reader's brain.'

Fernando Pessoa

CONTENTS

INTRODUCTION

I have a great deal of time for old Fernando, Portuguese writer and poet-inventor, whose gloomy multi-faced companionship in book form I now and then enjoy. I cannot, however, entirely copy his example (see dedication to this book); but at least my preface is mercifully short. I have saved you, in this summer edition of the *Superplonk* saga, from having to wade through a lengthy introduction to the book (unlike the winter edition). There are no introductions to the retailers either (again unlike the winter edition).

Why? Why am I so lazy? I don't have time for one thing, or the energy for another, or even the necessary inclination to write so much on the same subject twice a year.

This book is an updating of the previous year's *Superplonk*. In no sense is it a substitute for the winter edition to come. I agreed to compile a summer edition simply because of the incursion of so many new supermarket wines during spring; wines which demand early review; wines many specimens of which only last the summer; wines which require bringing speedily to the drinker's attention. Readers, as my postbag so richly testifies, wanted this book. I hope this answers the somewhat puzzling dig I came across in the *Hampstead & Highgate Express* last year, in an otherwise pleasing review of my work. 'A truly unpretentious wine writer is a rare beast, and Gluck is not just unpretentious but clear, straightforward and – sometimes brutally – frank. *Superplonk*, his survey of supermarket wine, starts with Asda and ends with Waitrose, giving the thumbs up or a pithy putdown to almost everything on the shelves. *Streetplonk* does the same for High Street wine shops, from Fullers to Wine Cellar. Quite why Gluck needs two books to achieve this survey is the one thing not made clear – perhaps it is simply that his greed is not confined to the grape.'

Why do I write two, indeed, three books a year, dear *Ham & High*? I'll tell you. It has nothing to do with greed. Indeed, I sometimes wistfully look back to the days, only really yesterday, when I just wrote *Superplonk* for the winter season and I had more time during the year for overseas travel (not to mention my two children). I write three books because readers want it that way. I have explained why it was necessary to have a summer update of *Superplonk*. *Streetplonk*, as a separate entity, is necessary because it deals with a very different breed of retailer for one thing and is bought by the reader with an interest in such shops. *Superplonk* was always a book dedicated solely to supermarkets and to add high street shops to it would double its cost and, for many readers, halve its appeal. Hence, two books aimed at two distinct readerships.

My readers, I never forget, give me my living. I am not a wine writer who thinks of himself as any grander than his readers; they know what they like, I do not quarrel with this and thus I am pleased, and indeed grateful, that there are drinkers out there who do not find my views on wine unpalatable, agree with the rating system I have devised, and generally find little disgusting in my recommendations. I sometimes feel I am simply a vast reservoir into which wine retailers pour their wines and out of which I fashion words for the thirsty Briton. From this I make sufficient to feed the family, oil my bike, go on holidays, and indulge certain passions (none of which, now that I think about it, is remotely extravagant – the odd bottle of impossible-to-resist wine and multi-coloured knitted jumper apart). My readers, I hope, enjoy a bargain-filled and healthy existence.

I have nothing more, at this point in the season, to add.

Except: joyous drinking to you!

Health Warning!

Health Warning is an arresting phrase. I hope by employing it I may save you from working yourself up into a state. Let me explain.

I get a few letters a week from readers (both column and book) telling me that a wine which I have said is on sale in a certain supermarket is not there and that the wine has either sold out or the branch claims to have no knowledge of it; I get letters telling me that a wine is a bit dearer than I said it was; and I get the odd note revealing that the vintage of the 16-point wine I have enthused about and which my correspondent desperately wants to buy is different from the one listed.

First of all, let me say that no wine guide in the short and inglorious history of the genre is more exhaustively researched, checked, and double-checked than this one. I do not list a wine if I do not have assurances from its retailer that it will be widely on sale when the guide is published. Where a wine is on restricted distribution, or stocks are short and vulnerable to the assault of determined readers (i.e. virtually all high rating, very cheap bottles), I will always clearly say so. However, large retailers use computer systems which cannot anticipate uncommon demand and which often miss the odd branch off the anticipated stocking list. I cannot check every branch myself (though I do nose around them when I can) and so a wine in this book may well, infuriatingly, be missing at the odd branch of its retailer and may not even be heard of by the branch simply because of inhuman error. Conversely, the same technology often tells a retailer's head office that a wine is out of stock when it has merely been completely cleared out of the warehouse. It may still be on sale in certain branches. Then there is the fact that not every wine I write about is stocked by every single branch of its listed supermarket. Every store has what are called retail plans and there may be half-a-dozen of these and every wine is subject to a different stocking policy according to the dictates of these cold-hearted plans.

I accept a wine as being in healthy distribution if several hundred branches, all over the country not just in selected parts of it, stock the wine. Do not assume, however, that this means every single branch has the wine.

I cannot, equally, guarantee that every wine in this book will still be in the same price band as printed (these bands follow this introduction). The vast majority will be. But there will always be the odd bottle from a country suddenly subject to a vicious swing in currency rates, or subject to an unprecedented rise in production costs which the supermarket cannot or is not prepared to swallow, and so a few pennies will get added to the price. If it is pounds, then you have cause for legitimate grievance. Please write to me. But don't lose a night's sleep if a wine is twenty pence more than I said it is. If you must, write to the appropriate supermarket. The department and the address to write to is provided with each supermarket's entry.

Now the puzzle of differing vintages. When I list and rate a wine, I do so only for the vintage stated. Any other vintage is a different wine requiring a new rating. Where vintages do have little difference in fruit quality, and more than a single vintage is on sale, then I say this clearly. If two vintages are on sale, and vary in quality and/or style, then they will be separately rated. However, be aware of one thing.

When *Superplonk Summer Edition* appears on sale there will be lots of eager drinkers aiming straight for the highest rating wines as soon as possible after the book is published. Thus the supermarket wine buyer who assures me that she has masses of stock of Domaine Piddlewhatsit and the wine will withstand the most virulent of sieges may find her shelves emptying in a tenth of the time she banked on – not knowing, of course, how well I rate the wine until the book goes on sale. It is entirely possible, therefore, that the vintage of a highly rated wine may sell out so quickly that new stocks of the follow-on vintage may be urgently brought on to shelf before I have tasted them. This can happen in some instances. I offer a bunch of perishable pansies, not a wreath of immortelles. I can do nothing about this fact of wine writing life, except to give up writing about wine.

Lastly, one thing more:

'Wine is a hostage to several fortunes (weather being even more uncertain and unpredictable than exchange rates) but the wine writer is hostage to just one: he cannot pour for his readers precisely the same wine as he poured for himself.'

This holds true for every wine in this book and every wine I will write about in the years to come. I am sent wines to taste regularly and I attend wine tastings all the time. If a wine is corked on these occasions, that is to say not in good condition because it has been tainted by the tree bark which is its seal, then it is not a problem for a bottle in good condition to be quickly supplied for me to taste. This is not, alas, a luxury which can be extended to my readers.

So if you find a wine not to your taste because it seems pretty foul or 'off' in some way, then do not assume that my rating system is up the creek; you may take it that the wine is faulty and must be returned as soon as possible to its retailer. Every retailer in this book is pledged to provide an instant refund for any faulty wine returned – no questions asked. I am not asking readers to share all my tastes in wine, or to agree completely with every rating for every wine. But where a wine I have well rated is obviously and patently foul then it is a duff bottle and you should be compensated by getting a fresh bottle free or by being given a refund.

How I Rate a Wine

Value for money is my single unwavering focus. I drink with my readers' pockets in my mouth. I do not see the necessity of paying a lot for a bottle of everyday drinking wine and only rarely do I consider it worth paying a high price for, say, a wine for a special occasion or because you want to experience what a so-called 'grand' wine may be like. There is more codswallop talked and written about wine, especially the so-called 'grand' stuff, than any subject except sex. The stench of this gobbledegook regularly perfumes wine merchants' catalogues, spices the backs of bottles, and rancidises the writings of those infatuated by or in the pay of producers of a particular wine region. I do taste expensive wines regularly. I do not, regularly, find them worth the money. That said, there are some pricey bottles in these pages. They are here either because I wish to provide an accurate, but low, rating of its worth so that readers will be given pause for thought or because the wine is genuinely worth every penny. A wine of magnificent complexity, thrilling fruit, superb aroma, great depth and finesse is worth drinking. I would not expect it to be an inexpensive bottle. I will rate it highly. I wish all wines which commanded such high prices were so well deserving of an equally high rating. The thing is, of course, that many bottles of wine I taste do have finesse and depth but do not come attached to an absurdly high price tag. These are the bottles I prize most. As, I hope, you will.

20 Is outstanding and faultless in all departments: smell, taste and finish in the throat. Worth the price, even if you have to take out a second mortgage.

19 A superb wine. Almost perfect and well worth the expense (if it is an expensive bottle).

18 An excellent wine but lacking that ineffable sublimity of richness and complexity to achieve the very highest rating. But superb drinking and thundering good value.

17 An exciting, well-made wine at an affordable price which offers real glimpses of multi-layered richness.

16 Very good wine indeed. Good enough for any dinner party. Not expensive but terrifically drinkable, satisfying and multi-dimensional; properly balanced.

15 For the money, a good mouthful with real style. Good flavour and fruit without costing a packet.

14 The top end of the everyday drinking wine. Well-made and to be seriously recommended at the price.

13 Good wine, true to its grape(s). Not great, but very drinkable.

12 Everyday drinking wine at a sensible price. Not exciting, but worthy.

11 Drinkable, but not a wine to dwell on. You don't wed a wine like this, though you might take it behind the bike shed with a bag of fish and chips.

10 Average wine (at a low price), yet still just about a passable mouthful. Also, wines which are terribly expensive and, though drinkable, cannot justify their high price.

9 Cheap plonk. Just about fit for parties in dustbin-sized dispensers.

8 On the rough side here.

7 Good for pickling onions or cleaning false teeth.

6 Hardly drinkable except as basic picnic plonk.

5 Wine with more defects than delights.

4 Not good at any price.

3 Barely drinkable.

2 Seriously – did this wine come from grapes?

1 The utter pits. The producer should be slung in prison.

The rating system above can be broken down into six broad sections.

Zero to 10: Avoid – unless entertaining stuffy wine writer.

10, 11:   Nothing poisonous but, though drinkable, rather dull.

12, 13:   Above average, interestingly made. Solid rather then sensational.

14, 15, 16: This is the exceptional, hugely drinkable stuff, from the very good to the brilliant.

17, 18:   Really wonderful wine worth anyone's money: complex, rich, exciting.

19, 20:   A toweringly brilliant world-class wine of self-evident style and individuality.

Prices

It is impossible to guarantee the price of any wine in this guide. This is why instead of printing the shop price, each wine is given a price band. This attempts to eliminate the problem of printing the wrong price for a wine. This can occur for all the usual boring but understandable reasons: inflation, economic conditions overseas, the narrow margins on some supermarket wines making it difficult to maintain consistent prices and, of course, the existence of those freebooters at the Exchequer who are liable to inflate taxes which the supermarkets cannot help but pass on. But even price banding is not foolproof. A wine listed in the book at, say, a B band price might be on sale at a C band price. How? Because a wine close to but under, say, £3.50 in spring when I tasted it might sneak across the border in summer. It happens, rarely enough not to concern me overmuch, but wine is an agricultural import, a sophisticated liquid food, and that makes it volatile where price is concerned. Frankly, I admire the way retailers have kept prices so stable for so many years. We drink cheaper (and healthier) wine now than we did thirty years ago. The price banding code assigned to each wine works as follows:

Price Band

A Under £2.50   B £2.50 to £3.50   C £3.50 to £5

D £5 to £7   E £7 to £10   F £10 to £13

G £13 to £20   H Over £20

All wines costing under £5 (i.e. A–C) have their price band set against a black background.

ACKNOWLEDGEMENTS

Linda Peskin, thank you for all your support with your computer. Sheila Crowley, Kate Lyall Grant, Jamie Hodder-Williams, Martin Neild and Karen Geary, my gratitude for publishing me and putting so much into this book. Felicity Rubinstein and Sarah Lutyens, my thanks for being such supportive agents. I must also record my debt to the members of the wine and press relations departments of the supermarkets listed who, though the cynic might protest that it's in their interests to keep old Superplonker sweet, are nevertheless often asked to go beyond the call of duty to satisfy my often pernickety requirements.

ASDA

ARGENTINIAN WINE RED

Argentinian Bonarda 1998, Asda   15.5 B

Juicy yet with a rich undertow of tannins, soft not earthy, and a hint of spice.

Argentinian Pinot Noir Oak Aged 1997, Asda   12 C

Possibly the least pinot-like pinot noir I've tasted in a coon's age. Make a lovely savoury jelly to accompany salamis and cold cuts.

Argentinian Red 1998, Asda   15.5 B

Such softly gathered blackberries and plums, a warm coat of unaggressive tannins, and a hint of leather and cherries on the finish. Lovely stuff.

Argentinian Sangiovese 1998, Asda   14.5 B

Juicier than any Chianti, this is teasing tippling.

Argentinian Tempranillo 1998, Asda   15.5 C

Gorgeous juiciness and dry tannins towed in its wake. Lovely texture and ripely ready fruit.

ARGENTINIAN WINE WHITE

Argentinian Chardonnay 1998, Asda   15.5 C

Very quiet but not subdued. The dry melon/nut fruit is elegant, not overstretched, and handsomely demure.

Argentinian Chenin Blanc 1998, Asda

A deliciously well-priced welcome-home-from-the-coalface-darling white of energy, crispness, soft underlying fruitiness and immense modern charm.

Argentinian White NV, Asda

Excellent value for barbecues and light fish suppers. A real sense of dryly purposeful fruit.

AUSTRALIAN WINE RED

Command Shiraz Elderton Estate 1993 `15` `H`

Sweet and savoury broth.

Hardys Cabernet/Shiraz/Merlot 1995 `14.5` `D`

Ribena School pay attention! This is your wine! You will love it! (So do I – a bit – but the sheer softness and sweet/dry fruit are very ripe and jammy.)

Hardys Nottage Hill Cabernet Sauvignon/ Shiraz 1997 `14` `D`

Hardys Stamp Cabernet Shiraz Merlot 1996 `15.5` `D`

Yes, it's juicy but there are tannins and tenacity. So: you get backbone!

Leasingham Clare Valley Grenache 1996 `15.5` `E`

This is improving nicely in bottle. Terrific sweet/rich, soft/hard, juicy/dry grenache.

Mount Hurtle Cabernet/Merlot 1995

Mount Hurtle Grenache Shiraz 1996

Oxford Landing Cabernet Sauvignon/Shiraz 1997

Penfolds Clare Valley Cabernet Shiraz 1996 (organic)

Very medicinal in feel.

Peter Lehmann Seven Surveys Dry Red 1996

Unusually couthly dry for an Aussie so-called-dry red. The biscuity chewiness, tannins and ripe fruit all attack at once. Not remotely over-the-top or over-embracing. Even delicate, in a sense.

Peter Lehmann Vine Vale Grenache 1997

Rosemount Estate Pinot Noir 1997

Takes nicely to chilling and drinking with seared salmon steaks.

Rosemount Estate Shiraz 1997

Rather raunchy and sensual in its aromatic richness and texture.

Rosemount Estate Shiraz Cabernet 1998

So deliciously sweet and fruity: soft and full yet delicate on the finish. Deliciously approachable and warm.

South Australia Cabernet Sauvignon 1996, Asda

AUSTRALIAN WINE WHITE

Cranswick Marsanne 1998

Dry yet with a hint of sticky richness. This is not a facade; it penetrates through to the fruit so food matches run the gamut from Thai squid to cod and chorizo.

Hardys Nottage Hill Chardonnay 1997

Ooh . . ! It oozes with controlled richness yet calm, insouciant, relaxed fruitiness of inexpressibly delicious firmness and flavour.

Hardys Stamp Riesling Traminer 1997

Hardys Stamps of Australia Grenache Rosé 1997

Karalta Semillon 1997, Asda

Bit dumb on the finish for a wine at this price.

Karalta South East Australian Semillon/ Chardonnay 1998

Clash of styles with the blend of grapes and this results in a pleasing texture and good tension.

Oxford Landing Sauvignon Blanc 1997

Penfolds Barossa Valley Semillon Chardonnay 1997

Love its richness and utter regality. It really lords it over other chardonnay blends.

Penfolds Organic Chardonnay/Sauvignon Blanc 1997   16 E

Quite superb level of fruit here: fresh, deep, dry, layered and lush without being remotely ungainly or blowsy.

Penfolds Rawson's Retreat Bin 21 Semillon Chardonnay Colombard 1997   15 C

Peter Lehmann Riesling 1998   15 D

Needs more time (two or three years) to really show us how deep and complex it is but that said this is highly drinkable now with subtle litheness and stylish-to-finish fruit.

Peter Lehmann The Barossa Semillon, 1997   15.5 D

Delicious bouncy richness with a faint lemonic undertone.

Rosemount Estate Semillon/Chardonnay 1997   15 D

BULGARIAN WINE   RED

Bulgarian Cabernet Sauvignon, Svichtov 1995, Asda   14 C

Bulgarian Country Red, Asda   14 B

Bulgarian Merlot 1996, Asda   13.5 B

Bulgarian Oak Aged Cabernet Sauvignon, Svichtov 1993, Asda | 15 | C

Svichtov Controlliran Cabernet Sauvignon 1993 | 13 | C

BULGARIAN WINE WHITE

Bulgarian Chardonnay 1997, Asda | 11 | B

Bulgarian Oaked Chardonnay 1996, Asda | 14 | C

CHILEAN WINE RED

35 Sur Cabernet Sauvignon 1998 | 16.5 | C

Superb cabernet of wit, warmth, character, concentration, softness yet dryness, approachability yet seriousness and a great potency of flavour on the finish. A vivacious cabernet of punch and pertinacity.

Araucano Cabernet Sauvignon 1996 | 13.5 | E

Chilean Cabernet Sauvignon 1997, Asda | 15 | C

Chilean Cabernet/Merlot 1997, Asda | 15.5 | C

Chilean Red 1997, Asda | 14.5 | B

Cono Sur Cabernet Reserve 1997   16   D

Concentrated and classy, it is in the class of the 35 Sur, which is a pound cheaper, and arguably has the more elegant tannins, but it doesn't deliver a pound more whack on the finish. But this is very compelling and high-rating wine.

Cono Sur Oaked Cabernet 1997   16   D

Superb dry edge gives the thrillingly soft, ripe fruit dignity and richness.

Gato Negro Chilean Merlot 1997   15   C

Pionero Chilean Merlot 1997   13.5   C

Rowan Brook Cabernet Sauvignon
Reserve 1994   13   C

Rowan Brook Oak Aged Cabernet
Sauvignon 1995   16   D

Deliciously minty and oaky yet very fresh and lively. Chile is effortlessly able to pull this trick off.

CHILEAN WINE   WHITE

35 Sur Sauvignon Blanc 1998   16   C

Superb! The grassiness of the acidity and the richness of fruit, still classic dry sauvignon, make for a wonderful crisp mouthful.

Araucano Chardonnay, Lurton 1997   16   E

Remarkably Californian style Chilean (i.e. elegant and very classy).

Chilean Sauvignon Blanc 1997, Asda   15.5 C

Chilean White 1997, Asda   14 B

Pionero Chardonnay 1997   15.5 C

**Rowan Brook Chardonnay Oak Aged
Reserve, Casablanca 1996**   16 C

Rich, woody, elegant, stylish, balanced, flavoursome, drinkable, good with food – what more can one say?

ENGLISH WINE   WHITE

**Three Choirs Coleridge Hill English
White 1996**   13.5 C

Three Choirs Madeleine Angevin 1997   11 D

FRENCH WINE   RED

Beaune 1er Cru Clos Roy 1990   13 H

Pleasant bitter edge. £22, though. Something to chew on.

Buzet Cuvee 44 1997   14.5 C

Chateau de Parenchere Bordeaux Superieure 1996 `15.5` `D`

Marvellous claret for the money: violets, blackcurrants (crushed and chewily rich and stalky) and earthy tannins of bite and bravado. A real food wine – chops, steaks, stews, cheeses.

Chateau Haut Bages Liberal, Pauillac 1994 `12` `G`

Interesting, serious and dry. Like tasting a dead librarian.

Chateau Peybonhomme les Tours, Premieres Cotes de Blaye 1996 `15.5` `D`

Chateau Vaugelas Cuvee Prestige Corbieres 1997 `15.5` `C`

Most controlled performance, if a touch dry/jammy on the finish, and it motors well over the taste buds with purpose and smoothness.

Chateauneuf-du-Pape 1997, Asda `13.5` `E`

Chenas 1997, Asda `14` `C`

Claret NV, Asda `14.5` `B`

Domaine de Picheral Bin 040 VdP d'Oc 1997 (organic) `14` `C`

Domaine Pont Pinot Noir 1996 `13` `D`

Gigondas Chateau du Trignon 1995 `15` `F`

Hale Bopp Merlot 1997 `13` `C`

La Domeq 'Vieilles Vignes' Syrah 1996 `16` `D`

A most compellingly flavoursome and vibrant syrah, with sunny fruit and earthiness but an underlying richness of great elegance.

Merlot, Vin de Pays d'Oc 1996, Asda `15` `B`

Morgon Michel Jambon 1996 `13.5` `D`

Moulin a Vent Oak Aged 1997, Asda `13.5` `D`

Oak Aged Cotes du Rhone 1997, Asda `13` `C`

Pauillac Bellechasse 1995 `13` `F`

Has some classic charm. But it's a bottle you want someone else to pay for.

Reserve du Chateau Mouton, Bordeaux Superieur 1997 `12` `D`

Has a decent, but delayed, finish of warm coal.

Tramontane Grenache VdP d'Oc 1997, Asda `15.5` `C`

Tramontane Merlot VdP d'Oc 1998, Asda `15` `B`

Great value merlot of a soft leathery tannic middle coated in ripe-ish fruit.

Tramontane Red VdP de l'Aude 1997, Asda `14.5` `B`

Tramontane Reserve Oak Aged Cabernet Sauvignon VdP d'Oc, Asda `14.5` `C`

Curiously dry on the finish when it is juicy and very un-cabernet-like as it makes its initial impact on the taste buds.

**Tramontane Reserve Syrah VdP d'Oc
1996, Asda** | 16.5 | D |

Superb Aussie confidence shaker. From Aussies in the Languedoc
this lovely rich, deep, aromatic, textured wine knocks many a
homespun Aussie wine into a cocked hat.

Tramontane Syrah VdP d'Oc 1997, Asda | 13.5 | C |

**Tramontane Syrah/Merlot VdP d'Oc
1997, Asda** | 14.5 | B |

FRENCH WINE   WHITE

Chablis 1996, Asda | 13.5 | E |

Chablis Grand Cru Bougros 1996 | 13 | G |

Lemonically limpid but twenty quid is a lot of money.

**Chablis Premier Cru Les Fourchaumes,
1995** | 14 | F |

Chardonnay, Jardin de la France 1997 | 14 | B |

Chateauneuf-du-Pape Blanc 1997 | 13 | G |

Hugely drinkable but fourteen quid? Difficult to fault as a well
balanced, classy tipple but . . .

Chenin Blanc Loire 1998, Asda | 12.5 | B |

Touch sweetish.

Hale Bopp Semillon/Sauvignon 1997 `14` `C`

James Herrick Chardonnay VdP d'Oc 1996 `14.5` `C`

La Domeq 'Tete de Cuvee' Blanc 1997 `14` `C`

Muscadet 1998, Asda `12` `B`

Not so crisp and dry as is typical. It will suit light fish dishes but it lacks punch.

**Oak Aged Cotes du Rhone Blanc
1997, Asda** `14` `C`

Pouilly Fuisse Clos du Chapel 1995 `12.5` `E`

Premieres Cotes de Bordeaux Blanc, Asda `14` `C`

Puligny-Montrachet 1995 `13` `G`

Classic touches of vegetality and finely knit texture.

Rosé d'Anjou 1998, Asda `12.5` `B`

Sweet – too so.

Sancerre Domaine de Sarry 1997 `13` `D`

St Veran Deux Roches 1997 `16` `D`

Always a most elegant performance turned in here: gently expressive of vegetal fruit, dry and satisfying and balanced. So much better a burgundy than scores more pretentious productions.

**Tramontane Chardonnay VdP d'Oc
1997, Asda** `14` `C`

**Tramontane Chardonnay/Vermentino VdP
d'Oc 1997, Asda** `15` `C`

**Tramontane Reserve Oak Aged
Chardonnay 1997, Asda** `14` `C`

**Tramontane Sauvignon Blanc VdP d'Oc
1997, Asda** `15` `B`

**VdP du Jardin de la France Chardonnay
1997, Asda** `14` `B`

Vouvray Denis Marchais 1997 `14` `C`

Delicious sour/sweet aperitif. Will age with great style for some years and acquire more points.

GERMAN WINE   WHITE

**Deidesheimer Hofstuck Riesling Kabinett
1997, Asda** `11` `C`

Devil's Rock Riesling Kabinett 1997 `14` `C`

Liebfraumilch Gold Seal 1997 `13.5` `B`

Wild Boar Dry Riesling 1996 `14` `C`

HUNGARIAN WINE   RED

Hungarian Cabernet Sauvignon NV, Asda   `13` `B`

**Hungarian Private Reserve Merlot
1997, Asda**   `15` `C`

Solid fruit of good texture, balance, ripeness yet not rowdiness, and a hint of depth from the rich tannins. Excellent glugging wine.

River Route Merlot/Pinot Noir 1997   `14` `B`

HUNGARIAN WINE   WHITE

Hungarian Irsai Oliver 1998, Asda   `15` `B`

Wonderfully dry yet curiously floral summer aperitif. Delicious with fish.

Hungarian Medium Chardonnay 1998, Asda   `13` `B`

Bit too sweet for a chardonnay.

Hungarian Pinot Noir Rosé 1997, Asda   `12` `C`

**Hungarian Private Reserve Sauvignon
Blanc 1997, Asda**   `12` `C`

**Private Reserve Hungarian Chardonnay
1997, Asda**   `12` `C`

ITALIAN WINE RED

Allora Primitivo 1997

Wonderful strident complexity as the wine flexes its fruity muscles as it flows over the taste buds – it shows many sides of itself including herbs, hedgerows and gripping tannins.

Amarone della Valpolicella Sanroseda
1993 (50cl)

Barolo Veglio Angelo 1994

Curiously antique in colour and fruit. Over-mellow and under dry, it seems sere before its time.

D'Istinto Nero d'Avola Sangiovese 1997

La Vis Trentino Oak Aged Merlot 1997,
Asda

A deliciously rich and vibrant merlot which will take terrifically well to chilling and consuming with food.

Montepulciano d'Abruzzo 1997, Asda `14` `B`

Montepulciano d'Abruzzo Cantine
Tollo 1997 `14` `B`

Piccini Chianti Reserva 1995

Old style Chianti at first sip, modern and juicy as it descends. Interesting wine to chill for barbecues when, such is its versatility, it will uncomplainingly accompany *everything*.

Puglia Toggia Rosso 1997, Asda ⬛16⬛ C

Lip-smackingly thickly textured, dry yet richly fruity, savoury yet glucose-tinged, wine of great deliciousness.

Sicilian Rosso NV, Asda ⬛13.5⬛ B

Valpolicella Classico San Ciriaco 1997 ⬛15⬛ D

Very juicy and ripe with a hint of spiced cherry and summer pudding. Great chilled as a personality-packed alternative to rosé. Good with food.

Valpolicella NV, Asda ⬛13⬛ B

ITALIAN WINE WHITE

Cantina Tollo Rosato 1996 ⬛14⬛ B

D'Istinto Catarratto Chardonnay 1997 (Sicily) ⬛14⬛ C

Frascati Superiore Colli di Catone NV ⬛12⬛ C

Dry and a bit dusty.

La Vis Aldadige Pinot Grigio 1997, Asda ⬛14⬛ C

La Vis Trentino Chardonnay 1997, Asda ⬛15.5⬛ C

Lambrusco Bianco NV, Asda ⬛13.5⬛ B

Wonderful sweet but far from sickly summer garden tipple for non-critical palates.

Lambrusco dell'Emilia Bianco Goldseal NV `13` `B`

Lambrusco Rosato NV, Asda `13` `A`

A summer thirst quencher for light-palated barbecue guests.

Orvieto Classico 1998, Asda `13.5` `B`

Good value if a touch reluctant on the finish.

Pinot Grigio Lis Neris 1997 `14.5` `E`

Terrific tenner's worth of lemon and apricot fruitiness. Real class here.

Puglia Chardonnay 1997, Asda `14.5` `C`

Sicilian Bianco NV, Asda `14.5` `B`

Soave NV, Asda `14` `B`

Soave Oak Aged NV, Asda `13.5` `C`

MALTESE WINE RED

Maltese Red 1998 `13.5` `C`

Juicy yet dry to finish. Odd ripeness to it.

MALTESE WINE WHITE

St Paul's Bay White 1997 `13.5` `C`

NEW ZEALAND WINE WHITE

**Timara Sauvignon Blanc/Semillon,
Marlborough 1997**
14 C

PORTUGUESE WINE RED

Bright Brothers Baga 1997
14 C

Douro 1997
13 C

PORTUGUESE WINE WHITE

**Bright Brothers Atlantic Vines Fernao
Pires/Chardonnay 1997**
15.5 C

Vinho Verde 1998, Asda
10 B

SOUTH AFRICAN WINE RED

**Cape Cabernet Sauvignon/Merlot Reserve
1997, Asda**
13.5 D

Again very juicy and chummy. I'd like it, at this price and
with a reserve tag, to be more reserved, complex, less obvious
and drier.

Cape Cabernet Sauvignon/Shiraz
1998, Asda `13` `D`

Very juicy and soft, and a bit too sweet on the finish. What happened to the tannins? Gone walkabout?

Cape Cinsault/Cabernet Franc 1997, Asda `15.5` `C`

Cape Cinsault/Ruby Cabernet 1997, Asda `14` `C`

Cape Merlot 1997, Asda `14.5` `C`

Cape Pinot Noir Reserve 1997, Asda `13.5` `D`

Cape Red NV, Asda `13.5` `B`

Kumala Cabernet Sauvignon/Shiraz 1997 `14` `C`

Landskroon Cabernet Franc/Merlot 1998 `14` `C`

South African Cabernet Sauvignon
1997, Asda `14` `C`

South African Pinotage 1997, Asda `14` `C`

SOUTH AFRICAN WINE WHITE

Cape Chardonnay 1998, Asda `13` `D`

Bit too cloying on the finish to rate higher.

Cape Muscat de Frontignan NV, Asda `14` `C`

Cape Reserve Chardonnay 1997, Asda `13` `D`

Cape Sauvignon Blanc 1997, Asda `14` `C`

Cape White 1997, Asda `12` `B`

Fairview Dry Rosé 1998 `16` `C`

One of the driest yet cheekily stylish and subtly fruity rosés on
sale. Bright yet restrained, firm yet fleshy – delicious contra-
diction.

Kumala Chenin/Chardonnay 1997 `13` `C`

SPANISH WINE RED

Baron de Ley Reserva Rioja 1994 `14` `D`

Touch pricey for dryness but good with food.

Don Darias Tinto NV `15` `B`

Terrific new-found polish and plumpness.

**Hecula Monastrell/Cabernet Sauvignon/
Merlot 1996** `16.5` `C`

Robust, rich, full of bite and depth, this wine is marvellous value
for money with its warmly knitted together fruit, chewy yet soft,
and full-blooded finish. Has character, charm, purpose and is a
treat for barbecued food (especially meats and vegetables).

Jumilla Tempranillo 1997, Asda `14` `B`

Monastrell 1998, Asda `15.5` `B`

Lovely broth of wine combining herby dryness with fruity

richness. It has a lovely baked edge of sunny warmth and the texture is outstanding for the money.

Oaked Tempranillo 1997, Asda `15.5` `B`

Rich, chillable fruit of lushness and litheness. Sure it's a touch ripe but it's never soppy or unrestrained. It has piles of flavour and style.

Rioja NV, Asda `14.5` `C`

Valdepenas Reserva 1993, Asda `15.5` `C`

Delicious, full, firm and fruity, it has a hint of a louche earthiness well held by the richly textured hedgerow flavours. A classy yet democratic wine of savour and savvy.

Vina Albali Gran Reserva 1991 `16` `D`

Terrific barbecued animal wine – anything from boar to Toulouse sausage. It's ripe, vanilla-tinged, dry yet full, nicely textured, warmly tannin-undertoned and very friendly. Better than many Riojas.

SPANISH WINE WHITE

Airen Spanish White 1998, Asda `13` `B`

Good with fish barbecues. Light and gently frilly on the finish.

Jumilla Airen 1997, Asda `14.5` `B`

Jumilla Macabeo 1997, Asda `13.5` `B`

La Vega Verdejo/Sauvignon Blanc 1997   `14` `C`

Dry, quirky, superbly fish-friendly, gently fruity yet lingering, unclassifiable.

Moscatel de Valencia NV, Asda   `16` `B`

Brilliant sweet wine for creme brulees, ice creams and fruit salad. Has a delicious undertone of marmalade.

USA WINE   RED

Arius Carignane 1997, Asda   `15.5` `C`

Arius Zinfandel NV   `10` `C`

Growers who nurture zinfandel fruit and go pink instead of red should be barbecued over slow fires.

California Red 1997, Asda   `14.5` `B`

California Syrah 1997, Asda   `15` `B`

So thick and clinging you could apply it to the tongue with a paintbrush. It tastes of baked plums. It will chill. It will be a conversation piece with barbecues.

USA WINE   WHITE

Arius Californian Chenin Blanc 1997, Asda   `13` `C`

**Arius Californian Oaked Colombard
1997, Asda** `14.5` `C`

Arius Colombard/Chardonnay 1997, Asda `14.5` `C`

Californian White 1997, Asda `13` `B`

**Chardonnay Kent Rasmussen, Napa
Valley 1996** `13.5` `G`

A lot of wood here. Hugely aromatic, and enticingly so, but the
tempestuous vegetality of the finish seems awkward.

FORTIFIED WINE

Amontillado Sherry Medium Dry, Asda `14` `C`

Fine Ruby Port, Asda `14` `D`

Not so much sweet as vibrantly, all-embracingly fruity and rich.
Terrific with sweetmeats and blue cheese.

Fino Sherry, Asda `14` `C`

LBV Port 1990, Asda `14` `D`

Tawny Port, Asda `15` `D`

Sweetish, yes, but the tea-leaf and nut edge relieves this impression and the finish is merely rich. Perhaps a winter rather than
a summer wine.

Vintage Character Port, Asda `14` `D`

SPARKLING WINE/CHAMPAGNE

Asti Spumante NV, Asda `11` `C`

For garrulous grannies only – it sticks dentures together.

Blue Lake Ridge Brut NV (Australia) `14` `C`

Blue Lake Ridge Rosé NV (Australia) `13` `C`

Blue Lake Ridge Sparkling Grenache NV `10` `D`

Cava Brut, Asda `16` `C`

One of the most elegant of the breed around.

Cava Medium Dry, Asda `13` `C`

Cava Rosada, Asda `15` `C`

Champagne Brut NV, Asda `13.5` `F`

Champagne Brut Rosé NV, Asda `13` `F`

Cremant de Bourgogne 1997 `14` `D`

Light and lissom. Very charming summer aperitif.

Nicholas Feuillate Blanc de Blancs NV `13` `G`

Nicholas Feuillate Demi-sec Champagne `11` `G`

Nottage Hill Sparkling Chardonnay 1996 `15` `D`

Three Choirs Cuvee Brut (England) `10` `D`

Veuve Clicquot Yellow Label Brut NV `11` `H`

Vintage Cava 1996, Asda `15.5` `D`

Touch more fruit than Asda's non-vintage Cava but not necessarily a pound's worth more of elegance.

Vintage Champagne 1990, Asda `12` `G`

Asda Stores Limited
Asda House
Great Wilson Street
Leeds LS11 5AD
Tel 0113 2435435
Fax 0113 2418146

BOOTHS

ARGENTINIAN WINE — RED

Libertad Sangiovese Malbec 1997 14 C

Mission Peak Bonarda Tempranillo, Mendoza NV 15 B

Mission Peak Red 13 B

Valle de Vistalba Barbera 1997 14.5 C

Lovely soft textured fruit.

ARGENTINIAN WINE — WHITE

Libertad Chenin Blanc 1997 15 C

AUSTRALIAN WINE — RED

Australian Red, South Eastern Australia NV, Booths 11 B

Brown Brothers Tarrango 1997 15 C

CV Shiraz, Western Australia 1996 13.5 E

Penfolds Bin 35 Cabernet Sauvignon/ Shiraz/Ruby Cabernet 1997

Juicy and well-meaning.

Penfolds Bin 407 Cabernet Sauvignon 1996

Seems a bit much for so modestly fruity, if impressively tannic, a wine.

Riddoch Cabernet Shiraz, Coonawarra 1995

Rosemount Estate Shiraz/Cabernet 1996

Stonyfell Metala 1996

Bit too juicy and cough-mixture-curious for any but lovers of oddities.

Tim Knappstein Cabernet Franc 1996

Wonderful concentration and richness here. Quite marvellous layered fruit – utterly superb and magically drinkable.

Wakefield Estate Cabernet Sauvignon, Clare Valley 1996

A big soupy broth but it has backbone and character and a huge depth of smoky, almost hammy richness of fruit. Great price for such Aussie splendiferousness. It is something 'rich and strange' and mildly tempestuous.

Yaldara Grenache, Whitmore Old Vineyard 1997

AUSTRALIAN WINE WHITE

Barramundi Semillon/Colombard/ Chardonnay NV

Cranswick Botrytis Semillon, Zirilli Vineyard, Riverina 1995 (half bottle)
15.5 F

CV Unwooded Chardonnay, Western Australia 1997
16.5 E

This is the year, '97, to wallow in the richness of the Aussie chardonnay, especially when no wood is aboard and the provenance is Western Australia. A gloriously uncluttered, elegant wine of potency, finesse and heavenly texture.

Deakin Estate Chardonnay, Victoria 1997

Unusual to find an under-a-fiver Aussie chardonnay so couth, civilised, classy and utterly delicious. Lovely texture and ripe, plump fruit.

Hardys Stamp Riesling/Gewurztraminer 1998

Terrific Thai dish wine. Hint of spice.

Ninth Island Chardonnay 1998
16 E

An expensive treat with its creamy depth and complex finish. Has a suggestion of old world vegetality but it is a triumph of cold fermentation and full fruit-retaining winemaking techniques.

Penfolds Clare Valley Organic Chardonnay/ Sauvignon Blanc 1997

Always one of the Aussie's most elegant white constructs, this vintage shows even surer grip than previous ones.

Penfolds Rawsons Retreat Bin 21 Semillon/Chardonnay/Colombard 1997

Superb fruit here, with loads of flavour yet that stylishness of tone and texture for which the '97 Aussie whites will become legendary.

Riddoch Chardonnay, Coonawarra 1996

Super mouth-filling plumpness of ripe fruit here, hint of caramel cream even, but the acidity surges alongside in support and the finish is regal. Very classy wine.

Shaw & Smith Sauvignon Blanc 1997

BULGARIAN WINE RED

Domaine Boyar Cabernet Sauvignon & Merlot NV

Quite brilliant: tannins, hedgerow, buckets of flavour and fruit – but also class.

Stambolovo Merlot Reserve 1993
15 B

Deliciously rampant fruit.

CHILEAN WINE   RED

**Carmen Grande Vidure Cabernet
Sauvignon, Maipo 1996**   `14` `D`

Cono Sur Pinot Noir 1997   `13.5` `C`

Tierra del Rey NV   `14.5` `C`

Controlled earth and rich plums.

Vina Linderos Cabernet Sauvignon 1996 `15.5` `D`

CHILEAN WINE   WHITE

**Cordillera Genesis Vineyard Chardonnay
1997**   `16.5` `C`

Superb value for such fluent plumpness, texture, vegetal polish
and depth of finish. Lovely wine.

**Isla Negra Chardonnay, Casablanca
Valley 1997**   `15` `C`

Tocornal White NV   `13.5` `B`

Via Vina Chardonnay 1998   `13.5` `C`

Curiously dry chardonnay for Chile.

FRENCH WINE RED

Bourgogne Pinot Noir, Joillot 1996   13 D

Interesting raw-edged burgundy. Has rampant tannins and a tetchy personality. But I like it (well, almost).

Bourgueil Domaine Pierre Gautier 1995   15 C

Crushed wild strawberry and shattered slate roof tiles. What a delicious mish-mash!

Cahors Cotes d'Olt 1997   15 C

Real country richness and nerve here. D'Artagnan bottled! Has buckle, swash, and some swish.

Chateau Ducla, Bordeaux 1997   15 D

Real claret at a lovely price.

Chateau l'Evziere, Pic St Loup, Coteaux de Languedoc 1996   15.5 D

Scrubland herbs and rich tobacco-edged fruit. Delicious.

Chateau Mayne-Vieil, Fronsac 1996   16.5 C

What wonderful claret! Lovely cheroot undertoned richness, great dryness, yet a compelling fruity finish. Sophisticated and svelte.

Chateau Pouchaud-Larquey, Bordeaux 1996   15.5 D

Delicious, organically farmed claret of richness and depth. Very dry but really concentrated and textured.

Clos Ferdinand Rouge, VdP des Cotes de Thongue
`16` `C`

Real class here – it purrs like a well-tuned engine: rich, deep, throbbing smoothly. A terrific quaffing and food wine.

Cotes du Rhone Villages 'Epilogue', G. Darriaud 1995
`13.5` `C`

Cuvee Aristide Haut Medoc 1996
`15` `D`

A richly textured claret of unusual plumpness of fruit. Lovely stuff.

Domaine Abbaye St-Hilaire Coteaux Varois 1998
`14` `B`

Dry, characterful, richly earthy and energetic. Will set any barbecue alight.

Domaine de l'Auris Syrah, Cotes de Roussillon Villages 1996
`16` `D`

The ultimate communion wine label, in one sense, and the wine inside, far from sacerdotal, presents itself erect, very dry, earthy and most rudely rustic.

Domaine du Trillol Corbieres 1995
`12` `C`

Domaine Pailleres et Pied Gu, Gigondas 1997
`16` `D`

Has what new world winemakers die to achieve: fruit with soul! Lovely richness and raunchiness here. Cool, elegant, characterful and deeply, decisively delicious.

Faugeres Gilbert Alquier 1996
`16.5` `D`

Makes an impressive case for *not spending* seven quid on an

Aussie shiraz. This wine is proud, rustic, tannic, rivetingly multi-textured and massively at home with food. It is the essence of a great French country red.

Fitou Mme Parmentier 1997 `13` `C`

Julienas, Paul Boutinot 1996 `12` `D`

La Reserve du Reverand Corbieres 1995 `15` `C`

Lirac, Domaine du Seigneur Lirac 1997 `15` `C`

The essence of deliciously earthy and herby Cotes du Rhone – lovely texture.

Marcillac 1997 `15` `D`

Very vegetal and herby; dry and decisive. Great food wine.

Oak-aged Claret Bordeaux Superieur 1996, Booths `14` `C`

Pernands Vergelesses, Cornu 1997 `10` `E`

Rasteau Domaine des Coteaux des Travers, Cotes du Rhone Villages 1997 `15.5` `D`

Delightful soft and gooey Rasteau – hint of floral herbiness.

Vin Rouge, Booths `14` `B`

FRENCH WINE WHITE

Bergerac Blanc NV, Booths `14.5` `B`

Bergerac Rouge, Booths `13` `B`

Berticot Semillon, Cotes de Duras 1997 `15` `B`

May have been replaced by the '98 by the time this book comes out.

Bordeaux Blanc Sec NV, Booths `13.5` `B`

Chablis Domaine de l'Eglantiere 1996 `11` `E`

**Chardonnay, Domaine Maurel VdP
d'Oc 1998** `14.5` `C`

Lovely dusky edge, quite rich and ripe, but stays dry to the finish which has some class to it.

Charles de Peregus, VdP de Tolosan 1997 `11` `B`

Humm . . .

Chateau Lamothe Vincent, Bordeaux 1998 `13.5` `C`

Chateau Pique-Segue, Montravel 1998 `14.5` `C`

Haughty, posh, very dry and crisply elegant.

**Cuvee Classique VdP des Cotes de
Gascogne Plaimont 1997** `14` `B`

**Dom Casteillas Rosé, Cotes de Roussillon
1996** `14` `D`

**Domaine de la Touche Muscadet sur
Lie 1996** `8` `C`

To be avoided, I fear.

49

Domaine St Jean de Pinede Rosé, VdP d'Oc 1997

May have been replaced by the '98 vintage by the time this book comes out.

Gewurztraminer d'Alsace, Cave de Turckheim 1997

Now this has some excitement with its rich, gently spicy fruit, redolent of crushed rose petals and fresh lychee juice. It has a bold structure of texture yet crisp underflow and it finishes with complexity and even a touch of extravagance. May have been replaced by the '98 vintage by the time this book comes out.

Honore de Berticot Sauvignon, Cotes de Duras 1997

Needs fish to spark it into life.

James Herrick Chardonnay 1997

One of southern France's most accomplished, classically styled, bargain chardonnays.

Joannis Rosé, VdP de Vaucluse 1998

Le Pecher Viognier VdP Vaucluse 1998

Apricot fruited, good viognier always are, and perhaps it's a touch fat but it isn't blowsy and it would be great with Thai food.

Louis Chatel Sur Lie VdP d'Oc 1997

Touch on the fierce side. Quel horreur!

Pouilly Fume les Cornets, Cailbourdin 1997   `10` `E`

Oh, what!

Riesling d'Alsace Amie Stentz 1997   `13` `D`

Sancerre Dezat Domaine de P'tit Roy 1997   `10` `E`

Dull, dull, dull.

Vin de Table Blanc NV, Booths   `13` `B`

GERMAN WINE   WHITE

Liebfraumilch NV, Booths   `13` `B`

Niersteiner Speigelberg Spatlese 1997   `12` `C`

Piesporter Michelsberg NV, Booths   `13.5` `C`

HUNGARIAN WINE   WHITE

**Chapel Hill Oaked Chardonnay, Balaton
Boglar NV**   `15.5` `B`

Cserszegi Fuszeres 1998   `14` `B`

Fresh, dry, fruity. Good value.

Hilltop Private Reserve Sauvignon Blanc 1998

15.5 C

Delicious mineral and sour melon edge to a really classy sauvignon. Can't afford Cloudy Bay? At a third of the price it's no mean substitute if not, obviously, so complex or concentrated.

ITALIAN WINE RED

Amarone Classico Brigaldara 1994

15 G

A great big soppy broth of a wine. Super-ripe grapes (cherries and spiced damsons) and rich tannin. A wonderful food wine.

Col-di-Sasso Sangiovese & Cabernet 1997

16 C

Superb savoury richness here: full, polished, deep, complex and dry. Classy and sophisticated.

La Prendina Cabernet Sauvignon 1996

13 F

Bit over the top for me.

Valpolicella Classico, Viviani 1997

12 D

Valpolicella Ripasso Viviani 1994

14 E

Gorgeously scrumptious fruit.

Vigna Flaminio Brindisi Vallone 1995

15 D

Rampant richness and ripeness here. Wonderful vibrant fruit.

ITALIAN WINE WHITE

Le Rime Pinot Grigio/Chardonnay 1998 `13.5` `C`

Le Vaglie Verdicchio 1997 `14` `E`

On of the most drinkable verdis I've tasted in the last five years.

Soave Classico Pra 1997 `13.5` `D`

Expensive, if highly drinkable.

MOROCCAN WINE RED

Moroccan Grenache/Cinsault 1997 `15`

Lovely warm fruit. It is literally bottled sunshine. You could get a tan just regarding the label.

NEW ZEALAND WINE WHITE

Lincoln Chardonnay, Gisborne 1996 `14` `D`

Vavasour Sauvignon Blanc 1997 `14` `E`

Old-style herbaceous Kiwi fruit.

PORTUGUESE WINE RED

Alta Mesa Red 1997 `14.5` `B`

Terrific posture! Sits up straight and true – muscled, lithe, fleshy.

Bela Fonte Baga 1997 `15.5` `C`

Terrific juicy fruit here. Delicious tarry richness and mature juiciness.

Foral Douro Tinto 1997 `13` `B`

Jose Neiva Oak Aged Red, Estremadura 1996 `13.5` `B`

Portada Red 1997 `15` `B`

Ripe cherries, crisp apple, mature plums – about do for you? (Does for me.)

Quinta das Setencostas 1997 `15` `C`

Elegant ripeness here.

Vinha Nova Vinho de Mesa `13.5` `B`

PORTUGUESE WINE WHITE

Bical Bela Fonte 1997 `15` `C`

Delicious steely specimen. Hard as nails. Oysters will love it – they'll go down singing.

Portada Estremadura White 1997

SOUTH AFRICAN WINE — RED

Heldeberg Shiraz 1996

Needs a robust lamb casserole to set it off. Or ripe cheeses.

SOUTH AFRICAN WINE — WHITE

**Altus Sauvignon Blanc, Boland Wynkeller
1997**

Jordan Chardonnay, Stellenbosch 1997

Big chewy white burgundy taste-alike. Great wine for chicken
and posh seafood dishes.

Landema Falls 1998

Welmoed Sauvignon Blanc 1997

Very very humourless. Perks up with shellfish, though.

SPANISH WINE — RED

**Casa de la Vina Tempranillo, Valdepenas
1998**

Casa Morena, Valdepenas NV

Cries out for rich food. Curries will make it.

Guelbenzu Jardin Garnacha, Navarra 1996

Mas Collet, Capcanes Tarragona 1997

The best red at Booths. Stunning complexity – deft, daring, delicious – combining blackberries and plums, hint of raspberry, with superb tannic incisiveness. Wonderful wine for the money.

Mas Donis, Capcanes Tarragona 1997

The second best red on Booths' shelves. Massively elegant yet richly characterful, it combines a medley of hedgerow fruits, deeply developed tannins and a compelling finish with a hint of spice. A wonderful wine of aplomb and presence.

Ochoa Tempranillo/Garnacha, Navarra 1997

So dry and daintily finished.

Scraping the Barrel Tempranillo, Utiel-Requena NV

Simply Spanish Soft Red NV

Quite revolting.

Vina Alarba, Calatayud 1998

Brilliantly constructed of sympathetic boots, plums, celery, herbs, cherries and a hint of dry earth to the tannins. Robust, soft, rich. Terrific with food.

SPANISH WINE · WHITE

Estrella Moscatel de Valencia

Either as a dessert wine or as a sweet, floral aperitif, this wine is brilliant. It is sunshine itself, packed into a bottle.

Mantel Blanco Verdejo-Sauvignon Blanc, Rueda 1997

Something different and dryishly witty.

Marques de Grinon Durius 1997

Dry but immensely self-assured and well-finished. Has polish and depth and a degree of finesse.

Santa Lucia Viura, Vino de la Tierra Manchuela 1998

Has a good form finish and crisp fruity attack.

Simply Spanish White NV

Rather flat on the finish. Needs to be blended with more rich fruit to give it extra wallop.

USA WINE · RED

Redwood Trail Pinot Noir 1997

Cherries and soft raspberry-edged fruit with a hint of tannin. Better than a thousand Nuits St Georges.

USA WINE   WHITE

Raymond Amberhill Chardonnay 1994   `16` `E`

Extremely rich and creamy with a hint of nuttiness and a
suggestion of vanilla and custard as it finishes. Very fleshy fruit
here with perhaps untypical lack of Californian finesse, but as
a brutal fruit lover, I like it. Great with dishes like spicy crab
cakes or coronation chicken.

Redwood Trail Chardonnay 1996   `15.5` `D`

FORTIFIED WINE

Amontillado, Booths   `14` `C`

Amontillado del Puerto, Lustau   `16` `E`

Sure, it smells mouldy and too ripe for comfort but imagine a
glass, well chilled, with a bowl of almonds and an absorbing
book. Great combination.

Churchill's White Port   `13` `E`

Crusted Port Churchill, Bottled 1988,
Booths   `16` `F`

Lush, rich, utterly extravagant in its commitment to sheer
pleasure.

Finest Reserve Port, Booths   `14` `E`

Fino, Booths `14` `C`

Henriques & Henriques 5 year Old Madeira `15` `F`

Manzanilla, Booths `14.5` `C`

Niepoort Ruby Port `13` `E`

Old East India Sherry, Lustau `16` `E`

Terrific molasses-rich fruit, gorgeous and sweet. Great with cakes and sweet biscuits.

Taylors Quinta de Vargellas Port 1986 `15.5` `G`

SPARKLING WINE/CHAMPAGNE

Argyll Brut, Williamette Valley 1989 (USA) `13` `F`

Bollinger Grande Anne 1989 `9.5` `H`

Champagne Brossault Rosé `11.5` `F`

Champagne Fleurie NV (organic) `10` `G`

Champagne Paul Nivelle NV `14` `E`

Chapelle de Cray Brut Rosé 1993 (France) `13` `C`

Good spritzer base.

Cremant d'Alsace Cuvee Prestige (France) `13` `E`

Deutz Marlborough Cuvee (New Zealand) | 15.5 | E

Palau Brut Cava NV | 10 | C

The first cava in some time I don't much care for.

Petillant de Listel, Traditional | 12 | A

Piper Heidsieck Brut Champagne | 12 | G

Seaview Rosé Brut | 15 | D

E H Booth & Co Limited
4–6 Fishergate
Preston
Lancs PR1 3LJ
Tel 01772 261701
Fax 01772 204316

BUDGENS

AUSTRALIAN WINE — RED

Australian Red NV, Budgens

They laid the fruit out in the sun and the vultures pecked it dry.

**Penfolds Bin 389 Cabernet Shiraz
1995**

Expensive muscle here. It's a bouncer of a wine: you don't get in without a hassle. Highly drinkable with food – spicy, rich, deep.

**Tarvin Ridge Mataro/Grenache
1997**

Wynns Coonawarra Shiraz 1996

Superbly classy and rich. Hints of mint cling to the deeply textured (denim and corduroy) fruit (plums, cherries and black-currants) and the sheer cheek of the fruit, its bounce yet gravitas, is terrific – the finish is syrup of figs.

AUSTRALIAN WINE — WHITE

Australian White NV, Budgens

Oh dear. Budgens' first own-label Aussie and it's struggling, at a middle-weight price, to punch its weight.

Brown Brothers Dry Muscat 1997 `15.5` `C`

Superb summer thirst-quencher and back garden aperitif. It is genuinely dry and classy and richly refreshing.

Loxton Lunchtime Light (4%) `13` `B`

Rawsons Retreat Bin 202 Riesling 1997 `15` `C`

Rosemount Estate Hunter Valley Chardonnay 1997 `16.5` `D`

It's the lushly controlled fruit, that hint of creamy, woody vanilla on the finish, that establishes its silky class.

Rosemount Estate Semillon/Chardonnay 1997 `15` `D`

Tarvin Ridge Trebbiano 1996/1997 `15` `C`

An utter curiosity, the 1996. Essential to have with food (anything from fish and chips to a monkfish casserole). It takes the dullest grape in Europe, lets it age (four years is late middle-age) yet provides sticky, dry fruit which will cling like liquid tentacles. The '97 is closely following on its heels.

CHILEAN WINE RED

Millaman Cabernet Malbec 1997 `13` `C`

Millaman Merlot 1997 `12` `C`

CHILEAN WINE WHITE

Vina Tarapaca Chardonnay 1997

A dry, wry wine of some substance and serious-minded demeanour – but the final fruity flourish is firm yet light-hearted. A classy wine.

CYPRIOT WINE RED

Keo Othello NV

FRENCH WINE RED

Abbaye St-Hilaire Coteaux Varois 1997

Soft yet hints of herbs and the Midi scrub. Superb, chilled or not, with all barbecued food.

Bourgogne Rouge Vienot 1996

Chateau Belvize Minervois 1996

Classy, austere, touch posh, very good value red for roast meats, cheese and vegetables.

Chateau de Malijay Cotes du Rhones 1996 `13.5` `C`

Bit austere and ragged on the finish.

Chateau Graulet Cotes de Blaye Bordeaux 1996 `14` `D`

Claret, Budgens `13` `B`

Corbieres Chateau Saint-Louis 1997 `13` `C`

Cotes du Rhones Villages Cuvee Reserve 1997 `14` `C`

A rich and very dry roast meat wine.

Cotes Marmandais, Beaupuy 1996 `13.5` `C`

Crozes-Hermitage Quinson 1997 `9` `C`

The wine inside the bottle seems almost as big a mess as the label outside.

Domaine Jean Fontaine Cairanne, Cotes du Rhone Villages 1995 `16` `C`

Superb balance and richness here: soft yet deep and dry, herby, scent of the hillsides, touch of earth – but overall terrific warm fruit.

Domaine St Roch VdP de l'Aude `10` `B`

Faugeres 1997 `13` `C`

Gargantua Cotes du Rhone 1997 `14` `C`

Not hugely Rabelaisian but drinkable, dry, hints of richness and a sound, firm finish.

Labretonie VdP de l'Agenais NV `15` `B`

Brilliant value for barbecues: has dryness and earthiness and thus immense food friendliness.

Le Haut Colombier VdP de la Drome NV `13.5` `B`

Listel Cabernet Franc, VdP d'Oc 1998 `16` `C`

An accomplished and deliciously uncompromising cabernet franc of dryness and richness. Superb touch of tasty tannins on the finish.

Pontet Saint-Bris St Emilion 1996 `13.5` `D`

Rouge de France Special Cuvee NV `10` `B`

FRENCH WINE WHITE

Blanc de Blancs Special Cuvee `13.5` `B`

Bordeaux Blanc Sec 1997 `13.5` `B`

Chardonnay VdP de l'Isle de Beaute 1997, Budgens `13.5` `B`

Chateau Lacroix Bordeaux 1997 `13` `C`

Cotes du Marmandais Beaupuy NV `13` `C`

Domaine Argentier Cotes de Thau 1998

Deliciously subtle: hints of ripeness nicely subsumed under fresh, firm fruit.

Domaine Villeroy-Castellas Sauvignon 1997

Superb grimly fruity specimen of high class, crispness, dryness and decisively well-structured fruit. It's very very sophisticated and as unashamedly French as D. Ginola's hippy swagger.

James Herrick Chardonnay 1997

One of southern France's most accomplished, classically styled, bargain chardonnays.

Laroche Grande Cuvee Chardonnay VdP d'Oc 1997

Macon-Ige les Cachettes 1997

Dry but very refreshing. The desert is dry, true, but it too is refreshing – as a break from routine. So is this wine.

Rosaline Cotes du Marmandais Rosé 1997

GERMAN WINE — WHITE

Flonheimer Adelberg Auslese 1997

Like licking a sugar-coated woolly jumper.

GREEK WINE   RED

Kourtaki Vin de Crete Red 1997   12.5 C

GREEK WINE   WHITE

Kourtaki Vin de Crete White 1997   14 C

Something dry for Greek food that isn't Retsina? This deliciously nutty, dry wine is it. Suits all fish dishes.

Orino Spiropoulos Greek Dry White 1996 (organic)   14.5 C

Samos Vin Doux NV (half bottle)   16 B

Brilliant value here. A rich, oily, waxy, almost biscuity, honey drenched pudding wine for the solo hedonist (in the useful half bottle) to get stuck into – and stuck is the carefully chosen word – as he or she attacks a block of foie gras, a creme brulee with fresh blueberries, or simply a goat's cheese with a bunch of fresh grapes.

ITALIAN WINE   RED

Avignonesi Vino Nobile de Montepulciano 1993   12 E

Merlot del Veneto Rocca NV   9   C

So spineless it can't walk.

Nexus Grave del Friuli San Simeone 1996   14   E

Primitivo Puglia Torrevento 1996   15.5   B

ITALIAN WINE   WHITE

Colombara Soave Classico, Zenato 1997   16   C

Superbly cool class and sophistication here. Strikes the palate
with huge style.

Frascati Superiore Casale del Grillo 1998   12   C

Verdicchio dei Castelli di Jesi 1997   13   C

NEW ZEALAND WINE   RED

Montana Cabernet Sauvignon/Merlot 1997   16   D

Deliciously combative stuff. Really works its way across the
taste buds with unstoppable tannins and rich leathery/black-
currant fruit.

Waimanu Premium Dry Red 1996   12   C

NEW ZEALAND WINE   WHITE

**Waimanu Muller-Thurgau & Sauvignon
Blanc 1998**

Getting better, this wine, with this vintage. More defined
and refined.

PORTUGUESE WINE   RED

Dao Dom Ferraz 1997

Rich, savoury, plump, spicy, ripe – it's deep and delicious and
great with grub.

SOUTH AFRICAN WINE   RED

Clear Mountain Cape Red   11   B

Helderberg Cinsaut Shiraz 1996   13   C

SOUTH AFRICAN WINE   WHITE

Clear Mountain Chenin Blanc NV   13.5   C

Helderberg Sauvignon Blanc 1997

SPANISH WINE RED

Diego de Almagro Valdepenas 1995

Very dry and arthritic – might be OK with a robust camel stew.

Marques de Caro Merlot 1995 11 C

Palacio de la Vega Cabernet Sauvignon/ Tempranillo 1995 17 C

Deep and dry and luscious. An utterly serious wine, at an amazing price for such woody complexity and maturity. It offers cassis, coffee, nuts and a touch of spice. A terrific wine.

Rioja Don Marino NV

SPANISH WINE WHITE

Moscatel de Valencia Vittore 14.5 B

SWISS WINE WHITE

Chasselas Romand 1996

UKRANIAN WINE RED

Potemkin Bay Odessa Black NV `3` `B`

URUGUAYAN WINE RED

Irurtia Nebbiolo 1997 `12` `C`

URUGUAYAN WINE WHITE

Irurtia Pinot Blanc 1997 `12` `C`

USA WINE RED

Angelo d'Angelo Rustica Sangiovese 1995 `12` `E`

California Red NV, Budgens `13` `C`

Has some tannins and a little oomph. Bit stingy on the finish.

Glen Ellen Cabernet Sauvignon 1996 `14` `D`

Stonegate Merlot 1995 `10` `F`

Sutter Home Zinfandel 1995 `13.5` `C`

USA WINE WHITE

California White NV, Budgens `10` `C`

Immensely dull and meanly fruity. This is California? Tastes like Iceland.

Stonegate Chardonnay 1996 `14` `E`

FORTIFIED WINE

Amontillado Sherry, Budgens `14` `C`

Blandy's Dry Special Madeira NV `13` `E`

Manzanilla La Guita `13` `C`

Marsala Cremovo Vino Aromatizzato all'Uovo, Filipetti NV `15` `C`

Rozes LBV Port 1992 `13.5` `E`

Rozes Ruby Port NV `13` `D`

Rozes Special Reserve Port NV `14` `D`

Warre's Warrior Port NV ‎ 13 E

SPARKLING WINE/CHAMPAGNE

Blanquette de Limoux Blanc de Blancs Divinaude ‎ 14 E

Brossault Rosé Champagne ‎ 11.5 F

Champagne Husson Rosé NV ‎ 11 G

Champagne Pierre Callot Blanc de Blancs Grand Cru Avize ‎ 12 G

Cremant de Bordeaux NV ‎ 13 D

Germain Brut Reserve Champagne ‎ 13 G

Lindauer Sparkling (New Zealand) ‎ 14.5 E

Expressive of nothing but great value for money and utterly charming sipping.

Mauler Sparkling Red Wine, Methode Champenoise NV (Switzerland) ‎ 10 E

They should really stick to yodelling.

Seppelt Salinger 1992 (Australia) ‎ 13 E

Budgens Stores Limited
PO Box 9
Stonefield Way
Ruislip
Middlesex HA4 0JR
Tel 0181 422 9511
Fax 0181 422 1596

CO-OP (CWS)

ARGENTINIAN WINE RED

Argentine Malbec/Bonarda 1997, Co-op `15.5` `B`

**Bright Brothers San Juan Reserve
Shiraz 1997** `15.5` `D`

Very jammy up-front but the tannins keep knocking at the door
and, finally, as the wine quits the throat, they are admitted.

Elsa Barbera 1996 `13` `C`

Graffigna Shiraz/Cabernet Sauvignon 1998 `16` `C`

Very potent and not excessively alcoholic (12%). Indeed it's
perfectly balanced and sanely fruity: tobacco, plums and smooth
tannins. Savoury with a suggestion of marzipan on the finish.
Terrific value.

**Marques de Grinon Diminio de Agrelo
Malbec 1997** `15.5` `D`

Lovely squashed fruit of richness with polished tannins.

Marques de Grinon Tempranillo 1997 `16` `C`

The sheer elegance and restrained richness of this wine are
superb.

Martins Merlot 1996 `12` `C`

Mission Peak Argentine Red NV `15` `B`

Terrific little party plonk: fizzes with soft, savoury, plummy
fruit with a hint of nuts and earth.

Weinert Malbec 1994　　　　　　　　13　E

Very fleshy and maturely developed (middle-age spread) and dutifully serious on the taste buds, deep and rich. Touch too old? Perhaps. And nine quid is too much.

ARGENTINIAN WINE　　　WHITE

Elsa Chardonnay/Semillon 1996　　　　14　C

Etchart Rio de Plata Torrontes 1997　　　13　C

Martins Chardonnay 1997　　　　　14.5　C

AUSTRALIAN WINE　　　RED

Barramundi Shiraz/Merlot　　　　　14　C

Hardys Cabernet Shiraz Merlot 1995　　14.5　D

Jacaranda Hill Shiraz 1997, Co-op　　　13　C

Leasingham Cabernet Sauvignon/Malbec 1994　　　　　　　　　16　E

This is what the Field-Marshal's boots smell of: gravy, leather, rich polish etc. The fruit is not so militarily correct but it is organised, bold and full of ideas. It's soft rather than firm, deep, developed and deft on the finish, and immensely drinkable with food.

Oxford Landing Cabernet Sauvignon/Shiraz 1997 — 15.5 | D

Delicious tobacco-scented fruit which though dry has a flowing, juicy finish to it. Well-behaved but has a hint of a dark past.

Oz Premium Australian Red NV — 12 | C

Personally, I can't drink it but it rates 12 because it isn't ugly or poisonous but curiously marzipanny and soupy in a way which some drinkers will love.

AUSTRALIAN WINE · WHITE

Hardys Chardonnay Sauvignon Blanc 1997 — 16 | D

Houghton Wildflower Ridge Chardonnay 1996 — 14 | D

Lindemans Bin 65 Chardonnay 1998 — 16 | C

Supremely sure of itself, this well-established brand showing, in its '98 manifestation, what a great year this is for Aussie whites from the region (Hunter Valley). This has great hints of warm fruit balanced by complex crispness and acidity. A lovely under-a-fiver bobby dazzler.

BULGARIAN WINE · RED

Domaine Boyar Pomorie Cabernet Merlot NV — 15 | B

Plovdiv Cabernet Sauvignon Rubin 1996 `15.5` `B`

The Bulgarian Vintners Sliven Merlot/Pinot Noir NV `14.5` `B`

CHILEAN WINE RED

Casa Lapostolle Merlot Cuvee Alexandre 1997 `17.5` `F`

One of the world's most delicious merlots, it is also stonking good value and unusually health-giving. A remarkable performer (for heart and soul).

Chilean Cabernet Sauvignon, Curico Valley, Co-op `15.5` `C`

Four Rivers Cabernet Sauvignon 1997 `15.5` `C`

La Palma Merlot Gran Reserva 1997 `17` `D`

Stunning aplomb here. Delivers its speech like Gielgud reading the back of a bus-ticket: fruity, soaring, arrogant, a touch disdainful, utterly and richly riveting.

Relativo Pinot Noir 1997 `16` `E`

A rather accomplished pinot with more oomph and pinot ferality than many a vaunted Volnay. It has ripeness and tannin, fruit and dryness, and a decent finish. A real roast chicken and wild mushroom pinot noir.

Terramater Zinfandel Shiraz 1997 `15.5` `C`

Unusual marriage and the partners fight a bit but this makes

82

for some interesting breadth as well as depth to the fruit. Needs food.

Tierra del Rey Chilean Red NV 15 B

CHILEAN WINE WHITE

Four Rivers Chardonnay 1997 16 C

Brilliance of tone, fingering, power and musicality. Great.

Tierra del Rey Chilean White NV 15.5 B

Vina Casablanca Chardonnay Sauvignon Blanc 1997 16.5 D

Has zip and vigour, serious depth, rich lingering fruit, a beautiful turn of litheness as it slides down the throat, and its overall confidence is world class. Available at Co-op Superstores.

CYPRIOT WINE RED

Island Vines Red Wine 1997, Co-op 13 B

Mountain Vines Reserve Cabernet Sauvignon & Maratheftiko 1997 16 C

Something a little different here: rich, dry, warm, herby fruit with a tang of the exotic about it: chocolate, dry cherries and plum, good tannins. Excellent casserole wine.

CYPRIOT WINE   WHITE

Island Vines White Wine 1997, Co-op   `13.5` `B`

ENGLISH WINE   WHITE

**Dart Valley Madeleine Angevine, Oak Aged,
1996, Co-op**   `11` `C`

FRENCH WINE   RED

Bad Tempered Cyril Tempranillo/Syrah NV   `14` `C`

**Beaujolais Villages, Domaine Granjean
1996**   `12` `C`

Bergerac Rouge, Co-op   `12` `B`

Claret Bordeaux, Co-op   `15` `C`

Cotes du Luberon, Co-op   `11` `B`

Cotes du Rhone, Co-op   `13` `B`

**Domaine des Salices Merlot VdP
d'Oc 1996**   `14` `C`

Fitou, Co-op `13.5` `C`

Minervois, Co-op `13` `B`

**Rivers Meet Cabernet Merlot, Bordeaux
1996** `13.5` `C`

Vin de Pays d'Oc Cabernet Merlot NV `15` `C`

Lovely texture to the wine, rich and deep and persistent, and the fruit levels off nicely on the finish to provide a hint of herbs and earth. But it's fruity and soft overall. Grand little glugger.

**Vin de Pays d'Oc Syrah/Malbec, Co-op
(vegetarian)** `13.5` `C`

Vin de Table Red, Co-op (1 litre) `13` `C`

FRENCH WINE   WHITE

**Alsace Gewurztraminer Producteurs A.
Eguisheim 1997** `16.5` `D`

What a delicious, rich, unpretentious, calm and collected gewurz we have here! Wonderful fruit (hints of lime, mango, lychees, rowanberry, papaya, guava – okay, only kidding) but it is faintly spicy and rosy rich. Superstores only.

**Angels View Gros Marseng/Chardonnay,
VdP des Cotes de Gascogne 1997** `16` `C`

Terrific marriage of the uncouth gros marseng with the hip international chardonnay. It's an elegant, individual wine of substance and wit combining the raw, almost spicy gooseberry of one grape and the rich melon of the other.

Blanc de Blancs Dry White, Co-op   8   B

Bordeaux Sauvignon Blanc, Co-op   13   B

Bourgogne Chardonnay Cave de Buxy 1996   13   D

Has hints of the vegetal glossiness of the grape from the higher region but not compelling enough for the money to rate higher.

Chateau Pierrousselle Entre Deux mers 1997   12   C

Domaine des Perruches Vouvray 1997   14   D

Vineyard of the budgies? Or the blabbermouths? Perruche translates either way depending which side of the street you stand. I stand firm at 14 points and the comment: 'Let it age three or four more years!'

La Baume Chardonnay VdP d'Oc 1997   15.5   C

Monbazillac Domaine du Haut-Rauly 1995 (half bottle)   14.5   C

Rose d'Anjou, Co-op   13.5   B

VdP d'Oc Sauvignon Blanc NV, Co-op   14   C

Vin de Pays d'Oc Chardonnay Chenin Blanc NV, Co-op   14.5   C

Modern, fresh, gently fruity, clean and excellent value. Boring testimonial? Perhaps, but chardonnay sometimes gets me that way.

Vin de Pays d'Oc Chardonnay NV, Co-op `13.5` `C`

Vin de Pays de l'Herault Blush `10` `C`

Vin de Pays des Cotes de Gascogne, Co-op `13.5` `B`

Vin de Pays des Cotes des Pyrenees Orientales, Co-op `14` `B`

Vin de Pays Sauvignon Blanc, Co-op `12` `C`

Wild Trout VdP d'Oc 1997 `15.5` `C`

GERMAN WINE   WHITE

Hock Deutscher Tafelwein, Co-op `8` `B`

Liebfraumilch, Co-op `10` `B`

Mosel Deutscher Tafelwein, Co-op `10` `B`

Ockfener Bockstein Riesling von Kesselstatt 1996 `14` `D`

HUNGARIAN WINE   RED

Chapel Hill Cabernet Sauvignon 1996 `13.5` `C`

Hungarian Red, Co-op `13` `B`

HUNGARIAN WINE WHITE

Chapel Hill Irsai Oliver 1997 `13.5` `B`

Hungarian White, Co-op `14.5` `B`

Hungaroo Pinot Gris 1996 `13.5` `C`

ITALIAN WINE RED

Sicilian Red, Co-op `12` `B`

Valpolicella, Co-op `13` `B`

ITALIAN WINE WHITE

Bianco di Custoza Vignagrande 1997 `13.5` `C`

Sicilian White, Co-op `13` `B`

Soave, Co-op `12` `B`

NEW ZEALAND WINE · WHITE

**Explorer's Vineyard Sauvignon Blanc
1996, Co-op** · 12 · D

PORTUGUESE WINE · RED

Portuguese Dao 1996, Co-op · 13.5 · C

PORTUGUESE WINE · WHITE

Portuguese Rose, Co-op · 10 · B

Vinho Verde, Co-op · 12 · B

ROMANIAN WINE · RED

Romanian Prairie Merlot 1997, Co-op · 14 · B

Sahateni Barrel Matured Merlot 1995 · 14 · C

SOUTH AFRICAN WINE   RED

Elephant Trail Cinsault/Merlot 1997, Co-op   `13.5` `C`

Jacana Cabernet Sauvignon 1996   `C`

Rich, perfumed, gorgeously textured, rampant but not wild, elegant yet not simpering or reluctant. A terrific, forward wine of great class.

Jacana Merlot 1995   `16.5` `D`

SOUTH AFRICAN WINE   WHITE

Cape White, Co-op   `12.5` `B`

Fairview Chardonnay 1996   `15` `D`

SPANISH WINE   RED

Berberana Rioja Tempranillo 1997   `15.5` `C`

Classic vanilla edge (American wood) but it's not too dry or sulky but silken and fresh.

Campo Rojo, Carinena   `14` `B`

Marino Tinto NV `14` `B`

Spanish Red NV, Co-op `10` `B`

SPANISH WINE WHITE

Albacora Verdejo/Chardonnay 1996 `13` `C`

Berberana Carta de Oro 1995 `13` `C`

Spanish Dry NV, Co-op `10` `B`

USA WINE RED

California Red, Co-op `13.5` `B`

USA WINE WHITE

California Colombard, Co-op `13` `B`

SPARKLING WINE/CHAMPAGNE

Freixenet Cordon Negro NV (Spain) `13` `D`

Brown Bros Pinot Noir/Chardonnay NV | 14.5 | | E |

Moscato Spumante, Co-op | 14.5 | | C |

Silver Ridge Sparkling Chardonnay Riesling NV | 13.5 | | D |

Co-operative Wholesale Society Limited
PO Box 53
New Century House
Manchester M60 4ES
Tel 0161 834 1212
Fax 0161 834 4507

KWIK SAVE

(subsidiary of Somerfield)

ARGENTINIAN WINE RED

Maranon Malbec NV `13` `B`

AUSTRALIAN WINE RED

Australian Cabernet Shiraz 1997, Somerfield `14` `C`

Juicy but more jaunty than jammy and so its swagger carries conviction.

Australian Cabernet Shiraz 1998, Somerfield `14.5` `C`

Rollingly rich and frolicsome.

Australian Dry Red, Somerfield `13.5` `B`

Australian Dry Red, Somerfield `15.5` `C`

Delicious! Delicious! Delicious! Did you get that? I said . . . oh, never mind.

AUSTRALIAN WINE WHITE

Australian Chardonnay 1998, Somerfield `16.5` `C`

Rich, smoky, developed, full and rich – hints of nut. Ripe but not too rampant. A lovely wine of great flavour.

Australian Dry White 1998, Somerfield

Superb value for money here, indeed astonishing: rich, fresh, classy, plump yet lissom, this is lovely wine of style and decisiveness.

Australian Dry White Wine, Somerfield

The cheapest Aussie white around? Probably. It is also the least typical and not especially dry. It's simple and sticky with a rich finish and is probably at its best with, indeed it *needs*, food like a Thai squid or chicken dish.

Lindemans Bin 65 Chardonnay 1998

Supremely sure of itself, this well-established brand showing, in its '98 manifestation, what a great year this is for Aussie whites from the region (Hunter Valley). This has great hints of warm fruit balanced by complex crispness and acidity. A lovely under-a-fiver bobby dazzler.

Pelican Bay Medium Dry White

BULGARIAN WINE RED

Bulgarian Cabernet Sauvignon 1997, Somerfield

Brilliant value. Not for the classicist perhaps but it's got lovely plummy fruit and firm tannins.

Domaine Boyar Lovico Suhindol Cabernet Sauvignon/Merlot

Domaine Boyar Reserve Gamza 1993

BULGARIAN WINE — WHITE

**Domaine Boyar Preslav Chardonnay/
Sauvignon Blanc 1996** `16` `B`

Khan Krum Riesling-Dimiat NV `12` `B`

**Suhindol Aligote Chardonnay Country
White, Somerfield** `14` `B`

Bit fresh: but fish will love its bony features.

CHILEAN WINE — RED

**Chilean Cabernet Sauvignon 1997,
Somerfield** `C`

Oh what nerve! It offers all of a great Bordeaux's tannins but
none of the austere fruit. It's simply terrific.

CHILEAN WINE — WHITE

Chilean Chardonnay 1998, Somerfield `16`

Woody complexity, hint of vegetality, persistence of rich fruit
and clean acids – is this a bargain or what?

Chilean White 1998, Somerfield   15.5   B

Thunderingly tasty bargain on all fronts: fruit, balance with acidity, class and fresh finish.

FRENCH WINE   RED

Cabernet Malbec VdP d'Oc 1997   15.5   B

Hints at sweetness then turns deliciously dry and a touch cheroot-edged.

Cabernet Sauvignon VdP d'Oc 1997   14   B

Claret Cuvee V E 1997   14   B

Claret, Somerfield   12   B

Corbieres Reserve Gravade 1996   16   B

It is the savouriness, the dryness, the sheer texture of the humid fruit. It's gripping and very stylish indeed.

Corbieres Rouge Val d'Orbieu, Somerfield   15.5   B

Terrific! Tasty, taut, tangy, tantalising! (Price suits to a T, too.)

Cotes du Rhone 1997   13   B

Les Oliviers VdT Francais Red NV   12   A

Bit like an anodyne cough-drop. I might marinate beef in it (or a pair of tired feet).

March Hare VdP d'Oc 1997   15.5 C

Lovely rich, dry fruit, herby, ripe and forward. Has developed richness and good tannin. Classy and civilised.

Merlot VdP d'Oc 1998, Somerfield   14.5 B

Most accomplished sense of balance between acid/fruit/tannins. Boring description? Yes, sorry.

Minervois Chateau la Reze 1996   16 B

Wonderful teeth-embracing tongue-curling, throat-charming fruit of style and wit. Fantastic value.

Morgon 1998   12.5 C

Rivers Meet Merlot/Cabernet, Bordeaux 1997   14 C

Very austere and proper – not pompous though.

Rouge de France, Selection Cuvee V E   13 B

Skylark Hill Merlot, VdP d'Oc 1997   15.5 B

Not a lot of leather, but a lot of love – terrific fruit here, soft yet dry, full yet elegant.

Skylark Hill Syrah VdP d'Oc 1997   15.5 B

Superb Cotes du Rhone taste-alike.

Skylark Hill Very Special Red VdP d'Oc 1997   14 B

St Didier VdP du Tarn 1997   15.5 B

FRENCH WINE   WHITE

Blanc de France Vin de Table NV   `15.5` `B`

What cheerful crispness and class! Astonishing . . .

Bordeaux Sauvignon Cuvee V E 1997   `13.5` `B`

Chablis Domaine de Bouchots Cuvee
Boissonneuse 1998   `12.5` `D`

Has some clean-cut elegance.

Chardonnay en sol Oxfordien, Bourgogne
1998   `14` `D`

Genuine white Burgundy. Hints of woodsmoke, vegetables,
vineyard.

Chardonnay VdP du Jardin de la France
1998   `14` `C`

Very fresh and knife-edge keen to finish. A wine for shellfish.

Chenin Blanc VdP du Jardin de la France
1997   `15.5` `A`

Wonderfully crisp and cheerful. Delicious lemon edge. May have
been replaced by the '98 vintage by the time this book appears
(not tasted as yet).

Les Oliviers du Jardin Vin de Table NV   `15.5` `A`

The best value white wine in the UK? Terrific, refreshing,
delightfully refreshing edge.

Rivers Meet Sauvignon/Semillon, Bordeaux 1997

Rivers Meet Sauvignon/Semillon, Bordeaux 1998

Very grassy undertone.

Rosé de France Selection Cuvee V E

Wild Trout VdP d'Oc 1997

Gorgeous ring-a-ding fruit combining freshness and fullness. Has elegance and bite.

GERMAN WINE WHITE

Hock, Somerfield

Mix with Perrier and ice for a lovely summer spritzer (15.5 points).

GREEK WINE RED

Mavrodaphne of Patras NV

As always, a real sweetie! Great with cakes and sweetmeats (and superb with Greek pastries).

GREEK WINE WHITE

Kourtakis Retsina NV

Brilliant value if you like, as I do, the musty tang of cricket bats.

HUNGARIAN WINE RED

Chapel Hill Merlot 1997

Stunning value for money – smells like a vintage Singer Hillman tourer (back seats only).

HUNGARIAN WINE WHITE

Hungarian Pinot Grigio, Tolna Region 1998

Utterly delicious back-garden thirst-quencher. Crisp in feel if not in finish, it has a delightful, subtle apricot edginess.

ITALIAN WINE RED

Gabbia d'Oro VdT Rosso

Merlot Venezie 1997 `14` B

Montepulciano d'Abruzzo, Venier NV `14` B

Solicella, VdT Umbria NV `15` B

Terra Rossa Sangiovese 1997 `16` B

Fantastic ripeness, clammy plums sweating richly all over the tannins, and the result is a gorgeous dry wine of great class.

Valpolicella Venier NV `13` B

ITALIAN WINE WHITE

Bianco di Puglia 1998, Somerfield `13.5` B

Gabbia d'Oro VdT Bianco `13` B

Pinot Grigio/Chardonnay Venezie 1997 `15` B

Sicilian White 1998. Somerfield `14` B

Richly flavoured and thickly knitted in texture. A barbecued fish wine.

Soave Venier NV `13` B

Terra Bianca Trebbiano 1997 `14` B

Villa Pani Frascati Superiore 1997 `13` B

PORTUGUESE WINE · RED

Falua, Ribatejo 1997 `15` `B`

Portuguese Red 1998, Somerfield `15` `B`

Great, soft, plummy thing! So cuddly and endearing and stuffed with fruit.

Vila Regia 1995 `15` `B`

Falua Red 1997 `15` `B`

Superb, gently earthy, plummy fruit.

PORTUGUESE WINE · WHITE

Portuguese White 1998, Somerfield `15` `B`

A proud fish and chips wine.

SOUTH AFRICAN WINE · RED

Cape Red 1998, Somerfield `15.5` `C`

What a wonderful house red! It may bring the house down but you will be protected. This wine is an elixir – it wards off evil.

SOUTH AFRICAN WINE   WHITE

South African Colombard 1998, Somerfield   14.5   C

South African Colombard 1998, Somerfield   15   C

Lovely melon/lemon double act.

South African Dry White 1998, Somerfield   14   B

SPANISH WINE   RED

Alta Mesa 1998   13.5   B

Bit tutti-frutti.

d'Avalos Tempranillo 1997   15   B

Flamenco Red NV   11   B

Los Molinos Tempranillo, Valdepenas 1993   15   B

Los Molinos Tempranillo, Valdepenas/Oak Aged 1993   15.5   B

Very ripe and tarry and delivers a lava-flow of warm, incandescent fruit.

Modernista Tempranillo 1997   16   B

Brilliant summer bargain for the barbecue! Has rich fluid fruit, developed and deep, and terrific tannins. Modern indeed!

Teja Tempranillo Cabernet 1997

SPANISH WINE WHITE

Moscatel de Valencia, Somerfield
Superb, rich fruit here, great with dessert, of cloying texture, candied melon, honeyed fruit. And a screw-cap too! No filthy tree bark!

USA WINE RED

E & J Gallo Cabernet Sauvignon 1997
Very juicy and a touch sweet.

E & J Gallo Ruby Cabernet 1997

USA WINE WHITE

E & J Gallo Chardonnay 1997
Dull, dull, dull – and it's dull (over-priced, over-hyped, over-engineered and, worse, over here).

FORTIFIED WINE

Fino Luis Caballero, Somerfield 16.5 C
Gorgeous bone-dry fruit: saline, almondy, tea-leafy – it's sheer classic Spanish tippling. Great with grilled prawns fresh from the barbecue.

SPARKLING WINE/CHAMPAGNE

Somerfield Cava Brut NV

Elegant, not coarse, taut, wimpish or blowsy, but has hints of ripe fruit and a restrained edge. Fantastic value.

Kwik Save Stores Limited
Warren Drive
Prestatyn
Denbighshire LL19 7HU
Tel 01745 887111
Fax 01745 882504

MARKS & SPENCER

AUSTRALIAN WINE   RED

Bin 201 Shiraz Cabernet 1998   `13.5` `C`

Very juicy.

Bin 252 Shiraz Malbec 1998   `14` `C`

Nicely tarry and dry with a jammy undertone.

Bin 312 Shiraz Merlot Ruby Cabernet 1998   `13.5` `C`

Very sweet and juicy.

Honeytree Shiraz Cabernet 1998   `13` `D`

So damned sweet!

Honeytree Shiraz Reserve 1998   `14` `E`

Some tightness to the fruit here. It doesn't slop all over the place
– like blackberries in a bucket.

**South East Australian Cabernet Shiraz
1997**   `15.5` `D`

Much better fruit here than other M&S Aussies: aromatic, rich
yet dry, soft, textured, tantalisingly tasty and well finished.

**Vasarelli McLaren Vale Cabernet
Sauvignon 1994**   `13` `E`

Absurd price.

Vine Vale Cabernet Shiraz 1995   `13.5` `E`

AUSTRALIAN WINE WHITE

Bin 109 South Eastern Australian Chardonnay 1998

Unusual Aussie richness tempered by some exotic acids to which I cannot put a name. Delicious texture and tension.

Bin 266 Semillon Chardonnay 1998

Superb blend of grapes presenting ripeness with freshness and dryness. Impressive concentration of fruit. Has ambition and accuracy. It seems to know exactly what it is doing.

Bin 381 Semillon 1998

I see no reason not to declare this a masterpiece – when smoked salmon is on the plate.

Haan Barossa Valley Semillon 1997

Honeytree Reserve Chardonnay 1998

Expensive for its hard-nose of freshness.

Honeytree Semillon Chardonnay 1998

Fresh and clean and a touch expensive.

Lindemans Bin 65 Chardonnay 1998

Supremely sure of itself, this well-established brand showing, in its '98 manifestation, what a great year this is for Aussie whites from the region (Hunter Valley). This has great hints of warm fruit balanced by complex crispness and acidity. A lovely under-a-fiver bobby dazzler.

Unoaked Chardonnay 1998

So plump and purposeful. It's delightfully uncluttered and beautifully, fleshily fruity.

Vasarelli McLaren Vale Chardonnay 1997

Lot of money.

Vine Vale Chardonnay, Barossa Valley 1996

CHILEAN WINE RED

Casa Leona Cabernet Sauvignon 1997

Goodness, the sheer chutzpah of the cassis fruit takes your breath away. A quite magical piece of fruit here of utterly scrumptious drinkability.

Casa Leona Merlot 1998

Wonderful sweet edge to hedgerow richness and leathery softness.

Casa Leona Reserve Cabernet Sauvignon 1997

Magnificent fatness yet daintiness. It's fully powered with vibrant tannins beautifully coated by the thick fruit. It's seriously complex, complete, utterly drinkable.

Casa Leona Reserve Merlot 1998

Savoury richness and polished plumpness. Lovely hints of new leather, herbs, hint of spice, and quite beautifully finished off.

Sierra Los Andes Cabernet/Merlot 1997

I love the dry, dusty, almost trail-weary edge to the wine which shrouds the rich, soft fruit in a complex cloak of dark, deep, slightly quirky individuality.

Sierra Los Andes Merlot/Cabernet Reserve 1997

More compacted, extruded, concentrated, and ineffably elegant than its non-reserve sister, it has more soupy and lingering richness – a touch. It is extraordinarily posh and vivid in feel. The texture is world-class.

CHILEAN WINE WHITE

Carmen Winemaker's Reserve Chardonnay, Casablanca Valley 1997 15 E

Rich and Aussie in style with a hint of California. Confused? Think how the wine feels.

Casa Leona Chardonnay 1998 15.5 C

Rippling plump with ripe fruit yet never too fat or immobile. It gently pulsates with dignified richness.

Casa Leona Chardonnay Reserve 1998 16 D

Vibrant, rich, balanced, very good value. The quality of the fruit is very high here. The balance incisive. The fruit and acidity offer depth yet deftness. Quite deliciously well-tailored fruit.

Sierra Los Andes Chardonnay 1998 `16.5` `C`

Superb burgundy-style vegetality incorporating new world touches of smokiness and buttery richness. Wonderful fruit really – almost contemptuous in its arrogant, easy richness yet calm.

Sierra Los Andes Chardonnay Reserve 1998 `15` `D`

Sierra Los Andes Gewurztraminer 1998 `14` `C`

Will age well for two years and this may improve and concentrate the imprint of the finish, which is slightly puerile. The perfume and entrance of the fruit, however, are terrific.

FRENCH WINE RED

Beaujolais 1997 `11` `C`

Bin 80 Cotes de Malepere 1996 `16` `C`

French country wine dragged deliriously into the late nineteenth century! Fabulous quaffing wine, characterful, dry, rich, sunny, gently herby, which is also a terrific food wine.

Bin 90 Minervois 1996 `15.5` `C`

Cafe Red VdP de l'Herault 1998 `14.5` `C`

Yes, it's juicy but the tannins help it get attractively past the finishing post. Middle-distance fruit, too.

Classic Claret Chateau Cazeau 1998 `13` `D`

Domaine Jeune Counoise 1998

Not as compelling as previous vintages.

Domaine St Pierre VdP de l'Herault 1998

Another juicy glugger but here there is a hint of tannin.

Fleurie 1997

**Gold Label Cabernet Sauvignon VdP
d'Oc 1997**

Superb jammy herbiness coated in thick rich tannin. Superb
little cabernet which shames many a fancy claret.

**Gold Label Cabernet Sauvignon/Merlot
Barrique 1997**

You think it's going to be another M&S sweetie whereupon a
nice, tarry dollop of tannins saves the day.

Gold Label Merlot VdP d'Oc 1997

Nice chewy duskiness to the fruit.

Gold Label Reserve Syrah Barrique 1997 13 D

Very ripe and juicy.

Gold Label Syrah 1998 13 C

Too rich and soppily sweet for me.

House Red VdP du Comte Tolosan 1998

Juicy!

La Tour de Prevot Reserve 1997

Lovely, rich, dark, jammy fruit of character and compelling drinkability.

La Tour du Prevot Cotes de Ventoux 1997

Getting too soft and juicy.

La Tour du Prevot Cuvee Speciale 1997

Very youthful, its character and depth have to be searched for. And time will help. It is ripe and responsive now, with classic Hermitage-like plumminess, but I think given a couple of years cellaring an 18-point wine might emerge. It has charm already and is rated thus, but the patient drinker (or, more accurately, non-drinker) may acquire an even greater treasure.

Margaux 1996

FRENCH WINE WHITE

Bourgogne Prestige Selection 1997

Calm, gently buttery and nutty, classic vegetal hints.

Cafe White VdP du Comte Tolosan 1998

Superbly nutty edge to some faintly exotic fruiting. Utterly delicious controlled richness and fresh, pineapple acidity. Terrific modern winemaking.

Chablis 1996

Hints of asparagus and hay here – but finely wrought and balanced. A very clean, decent Chablis.

Chablis Grand Cru Grenouille 1993

Yes, well, twenty quid's a lot of loot but this is a very fine wine of perfect maturity, subtlety, complexity and class. This is chardonnay in its utterly remorseless, clean, classic mode.

Chablis Premier Cru 1994

Wonderful sourpuss! Classic wine. Really sharply focused and concentrated chardonnay fruit of great finesse.

Chardonnay Merlot Rosé 1998

Odd specimen to find at M&S.

Cuvee de la Chapelle Muscadet Sevre et Maine 1998

Brilliant! Muscadet as it should be: utterly sushi-knife sharp (not tart), crisp, clean, mineral edged and demurely fruity. The best Muscadet I've tasted in ten years.

Domaine Mandeville Chardonnay VdP d'Oc 1998

Starts fresh and clean – it's the new M&S white wine trademark – then it goes gently oily and smoothly rich. Delightful, dainty, delicious.

Domaine Mandeville Viognier VdP d'Oc 1998

I've tasted Condrieus with less decisive gentility. A well-mannered apricot edge of fruit. Lovely stuff.

Gold Label Chardonnay Barrique 1998

Lovely controlled woodiness, subtle vegetality and calm, under-ripe melon fruit. Lovely burgundian style chardonnay.

Gold Label Chardonnay VdP d'Oc 1998   15.5 C

Superb haughtiness and high-minded fruit: it thinks it's a classic white burgundy.

Gold Label Rosé Syrah VdP d'Oc 1998   13 C

Very pear-drop fruity and adolescent.

Gold Label Sauvignon VdP d'Oc 1998   14 C

Very pert and properly po-faced sauvignon – that is to say, it's dry and very crisply turned out.

Pouilly Fume 1998   15 E

Clean and fresh with a hint of fresh melon.

Vin de Pays du Gers 1998   14 B

Utterly flawlessly fresh and simply stainless.

ITALIAN WINE   RED

Canfera 1996   16 E

Superb earthy balance here. Real class and complexity with marvellous warm tannins. A very accomplished wine indeed.

Chianti Classico 1997   13 E

Very jammy and super-ripe yet gently earthy underneath.

119

Ponte d'Oro Merlot del Veneto 1998   14.5   C

Pleasant, dry, cherry glugging. Delicious chilled with fish. Superb taint-free screwcap.

Ponte d'Oro Montepulciano d'Abruzzo 1998   16   C

Superb Italianate richness and dryness. And it's screwcapped. The wine's plummy and cherried, gently tannic and very taut. Lovely stuff.

Ponte d'Oro Sangiovese di Puglia 1998   15.5   C

Superbly fresh and bouncy yet fat and fleshy. Lovely texture and balance. A hugely gluggable wine of great charm. And it's screwcapped.

Reggiano Rosso Single Estate 1998   12   C

Very sweet and bubble-gum chewy.

Valpolicella Classico Single Estate 1998   13   C

Bit too juicy for me.

Vino Nobile di Montepulciano 1995   13.5   E

Supercharged dry ripeness.

ITALIAN WINE   WHITE

Frascati Superiore Single Estate 1998   14.5   C

One of the most classy Frascatis I've tasted.

Orvieto Single Estate 1998 `15` `C`

Delicious dryness yet gluggability here. Very accomplished sense of itself.

Ponte d'Oro Chardonnay du Puglia 1998 `14.5` `C`

Delicious screw-cap here – so no nasty cork taint. A terrific fresh-edged chardonnay of easy drinkability and versatile food matchability. Brilliant with smoked fish.

Sauvignon Isonzo del Friuli Single Estate 1998 `14.5` `C`

Curiously effective sauvignon with sticky rich fruit. Very good companion for rich fish dishes.

NEW ZEALAND WINE RED

Kaituna Hills Cabernet Merlot 1998 `13` `D`

Kaituna Hills Merlot Cabernet Reserve 1998 `13` `E`

Suggests it might have handsome stalky vegetality then goes all soppy on us.

NEW ZEALAND WINE WHITE

Kaituna Hills Gisborne Chardonnay 1998 `14` `D`

Kaituna Hills Reserve Chardonnay 1998

Very delicate complexity presenting smoky melon fruit with a hint of nut and a suggestion of minerality. Impressively well cut and stitched together.

Kaituna Hills Sauvignon Blanc 1998

SOUTH AFRICAN WINE RED

Bellevue Estate 1996

This has improved magnificently in bottle since I first tasted it and is now a refined, fruity treat, offering vigour and flamboyance, style and elegance, well-tailored but very very gently raffish.

Bin 121 Merlot Ruby Cabernet 1998

Cape Reflections Cabernet Sauvignon Merlot 1995

Cheek! To ask a tenner for fruity juice!

Oaked Ruby Cabernet 1997

Rock Ridge Cabernet Sauvignon 1998

Magnificent bargain here. The tannins and fruit offer smelliness (tobacco-edged), savouriness and a hint of spice, and that luxurious texture of ruffled corduroy. A smashing wine – good enough to grace the poshest and most highly polished of dinner tables.

SOUTH AFRICAN WINE   WHITE

Cape Country Chenin Blanc 1998   15   C

Drier, more concentrated that the colombard, this has some delicious sour gooseberry touches to its modernity.

Cape Country Colombard 1998   14   B

Very pert and fresh, hint of lime to the richness and it's a highly agreeable quaffing bottle.

Cape Reflections Chardonnay 1998   13.5   E

Finishes a touch ho-hum.

Perdeberg Sauvignon Blanc 1998   15.5   C

Rock Ridge Chardonnay 1998   14   C

USA WINE   RED

Santa Monica Classic Red 1998   11   C

Like Ribena – without attitude.

Santa Monica Zinfandel 1998   10   C

Too much sulphur in the bottle I tasted. The fruit was overmuch juicy too.

USA WINE WHITE

Santa Monica Classic White 1998

This is Californian? Well, well – or, rather . . .

Santa Monica Reserve Chardonnay 1998 13 C

Bit reluctant to curtsey as it exits.

FORTIFIED WINE

Pale Dry Fino Sherry

One of the best finos around, blended specifically to M&S's instructions, in which the bone dry salinity of classic fino has a background echo of gentle fruit so the result is a lingering pleasure, still very dry, of residual richness. A fino of exceptional style – and still a great wine for grilled prawns.

Vintage Character Port 15 D

SPARKLING WINE/CHAMPAGNE

Veuve Truffeau Colombard/Chardonnay Brut

Bluff Hill Sparkling Wine (New Zealand) `13` `D`

Cava Brut NV (Spain) `13.5` `D`

Cava Medium Dry NV (Spain) `12` `D`

Champagne de St Gall Blanc de Blancs NV `15` `G`

Classic.

Champagne de St Gall Brut NV `15` `G`

Best Champagne at M&S for the money.

Champagne de St Gall Vintage 1993 `13` `G`

Champagne Desroches Non Vintage `13.5` `G`

Some dry, classic touches.

Champagne Orpale 1988 `12` `H`

Silly price.

Champagne Oudinot Grand Cru 1993 `13` `G`

Lot of money. Too much.

Gold Label Sparkling Chardonnay 1998 `15` `D`

Delicious crispness and classic sparkling wine dryness. An excellent alternative to many champagnes.

Oudinot Brut Champagne `13` `F`

Sparkling Chardonnay Vin Mousseux de France NV `14` `D`

Vintage Cava 1994

More incisive than many a so-called great Champagne.

Marks & Spencer
Michael House
57 Baker Street
London W1A 1DN
Tel 0171 935 4422
Fax 0171 487 2679

Superplonk Summer Edition 1999

MORRISONS

ALGERIAN WINE   RED

Coteaux de Tlemcen 1994   `14.5` `B`

ARGENTINIAN WINE   RED

Balbi Barbaro 1997   `16` `E`

A treat for rich game dishes. The fruit is packed with flavour – from raspberries to spiced prunes – and the tannins are electric.

Balbi Shiraz 1997   `14` `C`

Cough linctus thick and very ripe.

Balbi Shiraz, Mendoza 1997   `16` `C`

Real Aussie shocker here: spicier, more concentrated, richer and more excitingly textured than an Oz likely lad for the same money.

Santa Julia Bonarda/Sangiovese 1998   `13` `C`

Very juicy/savoury fruit. Might be okay chilled with rich fish dishes.

ARGENTINIAN WINE   WHITE

Rio de Plate Chardonnay 1997   `13.5` `C`

AUSTRALIAN WINE — RED

Barramundi Shiraz/Merlot NV `14` `C`

Castle Ridge Bin CR1 Red 1996 `13` `C`

Corinda Ridge Cabernet/Merlot 1997 `13.5` `D`

Hanging Rock Cabernet Merlot 1997 `13` `D`

Hanging Rock Shiraz 1996 `12.5` `D`

Bit ordinary on the fruit (though I like the tannins) for seven quid.

AUSTRALIAN WINE — WHITE

Banrock Station Chardonnay 1998 `12` `C`

Like a boiled sweet without the sugar.

Banrock Station Chenin/Chardonnay 1998 `12` `B`

Castle Ridge Bin CR4 Colombard Chardonnay 1997 `13.5` `C`

Corinda Ridge Sauvignon/Semillon 1998 `14` `D`

Deakin Estate Chardonnay 1998 `15` `C`

The rampant richness is tightly controlled yet satisfyingly well-developed on the finish. Splendid price for such class.

Hanging Rock Sauvignon Blanc 1998   `13` `D`

Lindemans Bin 65 Chardonnay 1998   `16` `C`

Supremely sure of itself, this well-established brand showing, in its '98 manifestation, what a great year this is for Aussie whites from the region (Hunter Valley). This has great hints of warm fruit balanced by complex crispness and acidity. A lovely under-a-fiver bobby dazzler.

BULGARIAN WINE   RED

Boyar Iambol Cabernet Sauvignon 1998   `15` `B`

Brilliant dryness and wryness here. It seems so mature and serious yet it has great quaffability. However, it is a food wine.

Boyar Premium Oak Merlot 1997   `13` `C`

Bit juicy.

Bulgarian Reserve Merlot 1992   `14` `C`

Hidden Valley Reserve Cabernet Sauvignon 1993   `14` `C`

BULGARIAN WINE   WHITE

Bulgarian Reserve Chardonnay 1995   `15` `C`

Bulgarian Sauvignon Blanc 1996

CHILEAN WINE RED

Castillo de Molina Reserve Cabernet Sauvignon 1996

A stunning cabernet with piles of rich tannic fruit and cassis/chocolate undertones. A marvellously fluent yet dry wine of massive charm, depth, complexity and lingering fruit.

Chilean Cabernet Sauvignon 1998, Morrisons

Bargain cab which takes you from nasal charm to full-throated cosy fruitiness.

Stowells Chilean Cabernet Merlot NV (3-litre box)

Brilliant wine box fruit! Has depth, tannicity, richness, balance and bite. Great stuff. Price bracket has been adjusted to the 75cl equivalent.

Undurraga Merlot 1998

Vina Gracia Cabernet Sauvignon 1997

As with the merlot, Vina Gracia makes beautifully soft and aromatically satisfying wines of huge drinkability.

Vina Gracia Merlot 1998

Open, hearty, welcoming, rich, soft and leathery, this is an utterly luscious merlot of consummate quaffability.

CHILEAN WINE WHITE

Antu Mapu Sauvignon Blanc Reserve 1998

Combines a sauvy NZ-style freshness with an Aussie-style hint of rich opulence. Lovely food wine.

Castillo de Molina Reserve Chardonnay 1997

Luscious smoky richness, woodiness, softness and great balance. A lovely texture, aroma, solidity, finish and overall aplomb. Terrific value for money.

Chilean Sauvignon Blanc 1997

Montes Alpha Chardonnay 1996

Chile's greatest burgundian smell and taste alike? As if! This is better than any Montrachet I've tasted for twenty years. Except, of course, the great names (Comte Lafon etc). So – do you spend nine quid on this or £40 on a Lafon? True, the wines are different in mood. The Chilean has more verve.

Stowells Chilean Sauvignon Blanc NV (3-litre box)

Almost good enough, but not quite. Price bracket is the 75cl equivalent.

Villa Montes Sauvignon Blanc 1997

Crisp concentrated fruit with a lovely mineral undertone.

ENGLISH WINE WHITE

Three Choirs Estate Premium 1997

Possibly the most drinkable English wine.

FRENCH WINE RED

Beaujolais NV `13` `C`

Beaujolais Villages 1998 `10` `C`

**Chateau Cadillac Legourgues Bordeaux
Superieur 1995**

Superbly savoury tannins as ornate and complex as the gothic label. The fruit is tautologically blackcurranty and well spread and it packs a dry yet friendly fruity finish.

Chateau Jougrand St Chinian 1997 `12` `C`

Odd aroma of ripe compost-fruited grapes.

Chateau Le Fage Bergerac 1996 `14.5` `C`

Richness and dryness, scrubby fruit with good tannins.

Chinon Domaine de Briancon 1997   16   C

What a bargain! Tobacco and wild raspberries with gorgeous tannins, this is a classic Chinon of great wit and warmth, at a terrific price.

Claret, Morrisons   13   B

Coteaux du Languedoc NV   14.5   B

Lovely herby dryness and gentle, tannically coated richness. Great texture and savouriness.

Cotes de Luberon 1997   14   B

Cotes du Rhone NV   13   B

Cotes du Roussillon, Morrisons   15   B

Cotes du Ventoux La Pierre du Diable 1997   13   B

Falcon Ridge Cabernet Sauvignon, VdP d'Oc 1997   16.5   B

What staggeringly toothsome fruit here for the money. Quaffable yet complex, full yet dry, this combines cassis richness with marvellous tannins. A terrific cab.

Falcon Ridge Merlot 1998   16   B

Hint of ripe cherry and summer pudding but the tannins are so good and gorgeously rich the overall effect is of dry, serious, high class fruit. Huge charm.

Falcon Ridge Syrah 1998   16   B

Utterly resounding fruit – strawberries, raspberries and damsons – well baked and warm plus gentle meaty tannins. Overall, one of the most gluggable syrahs I've tasted, yet it has the heft to handle robust food.

Fitou NV `13` `C`

Gigondas Chateau St Andre 1997 `15` `D`

Big bonny bouncing fruit of lushly controlled meaty depth.

La Chasse du Pape Reserve Cotes du Rhone 1997 `15.5` `C`

Amazing price for such classy texture and richly rounded, yet gently earthy, fruit. A lot of wine for not a lot of money.

La Passion VdP Vaucluse Red 1997 `10` `B`

Le Pigeonnier Bergerac 1996 `12` `B`

Minervois Cellier la Chouf NV `13` `B`

Rhone Villages St Jean d'Ardieres 1996 `14` `C`

Gently jammy, warmly textured, handsomely smoothly-shaved and fruity.

Sichel Medoc NV `13` `D`

St Emilion, Morrisons `13` `C`

Winter Hill Red VdP de l'Aude 1997 `15.5` `B`

FRENCH WINE WHITE

Bordeaux Blanc NV `14` `B`

Chablis La Lotte 1996 `12` `D`

Chateau Le Fage Bergerac 1997 `14` `C`

Dry and charmingly wry, underfruited perhaps, but with a fat, greasy mackerel from the barbecue – perfect.

Chateau Loupiac Gaudiet 1995 (50cl) `15.5` `C`

Superb toasty, sesame-seedy, honeyed sweetness. Great texture and ripeness and lovely complexity. A great wine for sweet pastries.

Escoudou VdP de l'Herault Blanc 1997 `13.5` `A`

Falcon Ridge Chardonnay, VdP d'Oc 1998 `15.5` `B`

Fantastic value: real smoky, buttery, melon soft ripeness of fruit, gentle acidity, and thus a strident, dry yet rich finish. Terrific.

Falcon Ridge Marsanne, VdP d'Oc 1997 `14.5` `B`

The least convincing of the Falcon Ridge wines, made for Morrisons by Michael Goundrey (a benign Aussie), but still terrific value for such accommodating fruit. I suspect further vintages of this grape will improve hugely.

Falcon Ridge Rosé VdP d'Oc 1997 `14` `B`

Delicious cherry-fruited rosé of dryness and style.

Falcon Ridge Sauvignon Blanc, VdP d'Oc 1997 `15.5` `B`

Superb tenseness between fruit and acidity makes for an elegant sauvignon more satisfying at this money than many a Sancerre at twice the price.

Gewurztraminer Preiss-Zimmer 1998 `14.5` `D`

Soft, gently spicy, restrained richness, and brilliant with Peking duck.

Ginestet Oaked Bordeaux 1997 `14` `C`

Rather classy in a quiet way. Has touches of le vrai Bordeaux blanc: dry, gently pebbly and vegetal.

Haut Poitou Sauvignon Blanc NV `14` `B`

Interesting fish wine: nice fat grass-fed grapes, well chewed, make for a chewy, edgy wine.

La Passion VdP de Vaucluse 1997 `14` `B`

Very floral and perky and full of fruit. Bargain tippling for back garden pursuits.

Le Pecher Viognier VdP Vaucluse 1998 `14.5` `C`

Apricot fruited, good viognier always are, and perhaps it's a touch fat but it isn't blowsy and it would be great with Thai food.

'M' Muscadet Sevre et Maine `12` `B`

Macon Villages Teissedre 1998 `13` `C`

Touch uncertain on the finish.

Rosé d'Anjou, Morrisons `14` `B`

Saint Veran Pierre Thomas 1997 14 D

Soft and stylish. A decent white burgundy at a decent price.

Winter Hill White 1997 15.5 B

GERMAN WINE WHITE

Bereich Bernkastel 1996 11 B

Franz Reh Auslese 1997 14 C

Delicious honeyed summer, well-chilled aperitif – or try it as a spritzer ingredient.

Kendermanns Dry Riesling 1997 13 C

Klussterather St Michael Spatlese 1996 11.5 C

'M' Mosel Light & Flinty 11 B

Wehlener Sonnenuhr Riesling Spatlese 1997 11 D

Very sweet and one-sided.

Zimmermann Bereich Bernkastel Rivaner 1997 10 B

Zimmermann Riesling NV 13 C

GREEK WINE RED

Boutari Xinomavro 1995 `14` `E`

Mavrodaphne of Patras `14` `C`

HUNGARIAN WINE RED

Chapel Hill Pinot Noir `10` `B`

HUNGARIAN WINE WHITE

Chapel Hill Irsai Oliver `13.5` `B`

River Duna Chardonnay 1997 `13` `C`

River Duna Gewurztraminer 1997 `12` `B`

ITALIAN WINE RED

Barbera Piemonte 1997 `12` `B`

Casa di Monzi Merlot 1997 `12` `C`

Chianti Uggiano 1996 `14` `C`

**Falconeri Cabernet Sauvignon di Toscana
Uggiano 1995** `13.5` `F`

A lovely tannic wine, touch of baked rich fruit, but thirteen quid
takes a lot of thinking about. If the wine provided concomitant
fruity complexity, in spite of its undoubted quality, I would rate
it higher. But I can't.

La Quercie Montepulciano Uggiano 1996 `14` `C`

Montepulciano d'Abruzzo 1997 `15` `B`

Valpolicella NV `12` `B`

Vino Rosso di Puglia NV `10` `B`

Fruit juice.

ITALIAN WINE WHITE

Casa de Monzi Chardonnay 1997 `15.5` `C`

Curiously dry and palate-stretching on the finish from an
entrance which is bold and softly striking. Very convincing
chardonnay.

Chardonnay di Puglia NV `13` `B`

Ritratti Pinot Grigio Trentino 1997 `15.5` `D`

Delicious change from chardonnay. Here it isn't cheap but
gamine and good-hearted, rich, deep and brilliant with food.

Segesta Italian White 1997 `14.5` `C`

Elegant, rich, balanced, aromatic, brilliant value.

Soave NV `13` `B`

MEXICAN WINE RED

L A Cetto Zinfandel 1997 `C`

Bit anodyne for Cetto. Where's the raw, dry spark of thorny zin fruit?

MOROCCAN WINE RED

Le Chameau Grenache Cinsault NV `11` `B`

Terribly terribly juicy.

NEW ZEALAND WINE WHITE

Canterbury House Chardonnay 1997 `D`

Dull.

Canterbury House Riesling 1997 11 D

Canterbury House Sauvignon Blanc 1997 12 D

Grassy and ragged with it. No finely manicured lawn here.

**Whitecliff Sacred Hill Sauvignon Blanc
1997** 10 C

PORTUGUESE WINE RED

Dao Meia Encosta 1996 14 C

PORTUGUESE WINE WHITE

Vinho Verde 10 B

ROMANIAN WINE RED

**'M' Ideal with Friends Cabernet Sauvignon
1997** 14 B

Nicely tannic and savoury. One's friends need to have dry palates
and fruity dispositions.

Romanian Border Pinot Noir 1995 `15` `B`

Romanian Country Red `12` `B`

ROMANIAN WINE WHITE

Late Harvest Chardonnay 1987 (yes, 1987!) `13.5` `C`

Curious pastry-edged fruit-tart fruit. Will it accompany such a dessert? Hmm . . .

SOUTH AFRICAN WINE RED

Cathedral Cellars Merlot 1996 `13` `E`

Bit juicy for eight quid.

Kleindal Pinotage 1997   `C`

Terrific value for meaty barbecues. The tannins are hair-raisingly rich and active.

Neil Joubert Cabernet Sauvignon 1997 `13` `C`

Very soft and slippery – you only catch it if you concentrate hard.

South African Red NV   `B`

SOUTH AFRICAN WINE · WHITE

Black Wood Chenin Blanc 1998 `14.5` `B`

Great value fish wine. Dry and mineral-edged.

Dukesfield Chardonnay 1997 `13.5` `C`

'M' South African White Crisp and Fruity `13.5` `B`

SPANISH WINE · RED

Chateldon Cabernet Sauvignon Reserva 1994 `15` `C`

Good Spanish Red `13.5` `B`

Remonte Crianza Cabernet Sauvignon, Navarra 1996 `14.5` `C`

Juicy with hints of warm cheroot. Great glugging here.

Rio Rojo Tinto NV `14` `B`

A light and versatile red which can be drunk with casseroles or chilled to accommodate barbecued fish.

Rioja NV, Morrisons `16` `C`

Great vanilla-edged ripeness and richness. Full, deep, balanced and deliciously fruity.

Stowells Tempranillo NV (3-litre box) `12.5` `B`

Price bracket has been adjusted to the 75cl equivalent.

Torres Sangre de Toro 1996 `15.5` `C`

In great form, this old bull of a wine. Has firm tannins undercoating rich, gently jammy fruit. Hugely drinkable.

SPANISH WINE WHITE

Torres Vina Sol 1998 `13` `C`

USA WINE RED

Blossom Hill California Red NV `10` `C`

Extremely juicy and synthetic.

Californian Red NV `13` `B`

Glen Ellen Proprietor's Reserve Zinfandel 1997 `12` `C`

Slips down well, without leaving a huge impression.

Ironstone Cabernet Franc 1996 `14` `D`

Starts well with a lovely stalky aroma, lots of rich sweet fruit and dry tannins making for balance. Finishes fruitily and without complexity.

Murieta's Well, Livermore Valley 1995

USA WINE   WHITE

Blossom Hill White Zinfandel Rosé 1997

Those who commit the heresy of making rosé from zinfandel grapes have only Hell to look forward to when hot irons will apply eternal torture.

Californian White NV

Ironstone Chardonnay 1997

Lovely rich fruit, polished and buttery, and with great litheness. It's a muscular yet very spry wine of depth and decisiveness. Very good price.

Mission Hill Chardonnay Reserve 1996

Drinkable and almost very fine. But lacks punch on the finish for a tenner and it isn't especially complex.

Talus Chardonnay 1995

Gorgeous rich, ripe fruit combining dry, sticky-toffee texture with huge dollops of melon and pear.

Wente Chenin Blanc, Le Blanc de Blanc 1997

Again, a Wente which is rich, almost sweetish, and not subtle but with Thai fish cakes, herby and heavy, I can't think of anything better for the money.

USA WHITE

Wente Johannesburg Riesling 1996   `16` `C`

Superb rich fruit here, absolutely full of itself, true, but has
bounce, has creamy depth, is great for reviving quaffing and
for oriental food.

FORTIFIED WINE

Rozes Special Reserve Port NV   `14` `D`

SPARKLING WINE/CHAMPAGNE

Asti Spumante Gianni (Italian)   `14` `C`

Chapel Hill Chardonnay-Pinot Noir NV
(Hungary)   `12` `C`

Bit numb.

Millennium Cava 1996   `14` `E`

Rich yet restrained, dry yet mouth-filling, classy and confident.

Nicole d'Aurigny Brut Champagne   `14` `E`

Paul Herard Champagne Brut NV   `12` `F`

Paul Herard Demi Sec Champagne
(half bottle)   `13.5` `D`

Rondel Cava Rosé   14 D

**Santa Carolina Chardonnay Brut 1996
(Chile)**   14 D

A fruity bubbly which is not remotely champagne-like in
its style.

Seaview Brut NV (Australia)   14 D

Lithe and light. Delicious simplicity.

Seaview Brut Rosé (Australia)   15 D

Sparkling Zero (alcohol free)   15 A

Wm Morrisons Supermarkets
Wakefield 41 Industrial Estate
Wakefield
W Yorks WFl 0XF
Tel 01924 870000
Fax 01924 921250

SAFEWAY

ARGENTINIAN WINE RED

Balbi Malbec 1998 `14` `C`

Very fat and fulsome. Great with food.

Caballo de Plata Bonarda-Barbera 1998 `13` `B`

Intensely soft and juicy. Might do a brinjal and curried rice proud.

Diego Murillo Malbec, Patagonia 1997 `17` `D`

Fabulous roast fowl wine. Combines rich baked spicy fruit and evolved tannins. Incredible richness.

Fantelli Barbera/Cabernet, Mendoza 1998 `16.5` `C`

Bargain bonny red combining ripe, textured fruit and structured richness.

Mendoza Merlot 1997, Safeway `13.5` `C`

Rafael Estate Malbec, Mendoza 1997 `16` `D`

Good heavens what nerve! It's the cheekiest amalgam of fruit and tannin I've tasted for years. Top 212 stores.

Santa Ana Cabernet/Malbec, Mendoza 1997 `14.5` `C`

ARGENTINIAN WINE WHITE

Alamos Ridge Chardonnay, Mendoza 1996 `15.5` `D`

Caballo de Plata Torrontes 1998 `12` `B`

Rafael Estate Chardonnay/Chenin, Mendoza 1997 `14.5` `C`

Santa Ana Chardonnay/Semillon, Mendoza 1997 `15.5` `C`

Santa Ana Malbec Rosé 1998 `14` `C`

A very rich dry rosé of some weight and serious food compatibility.

AUSTRALIAN WINE RED

Australian Oaked Cabernet Sauvignon 1998, Safeway `16` `C`

Seems to hint at ripeness and juiciness but the lovely soft tannins cruise in and take command.

Australian Oaked Shiraz 1998, Safeway `14` `C`

Smoky rubbery fruit, hint of vegetality, good tannins, rich polish.

Australian Shiraz 1997, Safeway `13` `C`

Australian Shiraz/Ruby Cabernet 1998, Safeway `13.5` `C`

Highly cooked and rich. Like a gravy for roast grouse.

Capel Vale Shiraz 1997 `13.5` `E`

Top 130 stores.

**Chateau Reynella Basket-Pressed
Shiraz 1995** `15.5` `F`

Conundrum Vineyards Shiraz/Malbec 1997 `12` `D`

Like fruit juice – without attitude.

Dawn Ridge Australian Red (3-litre box) `15` `B`

**Hardys Coonawarra Cabernet Sauvignon
1995** `15.5` `E`

Jacob's Creek Grenache Shiraz 1998 `14` `C`

Raunchy, restless and deeply engaging.

Knappstein Cabernet Franc 1996 `16.5` `E`

Wonderful concentration and richness here. Quite marvellous
layered fruit – utterly superb and magically drinkable. Top
130 stores.

Knappstein Cabernet/Merlot 1996 `13.5` `E`

Too juicy for eight quid. Top 130 stores.

Mamre Brook Cabernet Sauvignon 1996 `16` `E`

Now here the juice of the blackcurrants is firmly textured by
great tannins. Top thirty-six stores.

**McPherson Croftwood Vineyard Shiraz,
SE Australia 1998** `15` `C`

Metala Shiraz/Cabernet Sauvignon 1997

Top 130 stores.

Normans Old Vine Shiraz 1997

Like a medicine for thin nonagenarians. Top forty stores from mid-June.

Penfolds Bin 389 Cabernet Shiraz 1996

Sufficient unto itself. Settle down with a rich, tannic author and relish the intricate plot of this stunning wine. Top thirty-six stores.

Peter Lehmann The Barossa Cabernet Sauvignon 1996

Fabulously good value for an Aussie nowadays: dry, balanced, witty, rich, lengthy, deep and fully dimensional. Great stuff.

Rosemount Estate Show Reserve Cabernet Sauvignon 1996

Too juicy and characterless for fifteen quid. Top thirty-six stores.

Taltarni Merlot/Cabernet Sauvignon 1997

Curiously dry for an Aussie red. Classic touches of Bordeaux! Top 130 stores.

Woolshed Cabernet/Shiraz/Merlot, Coonawarra 1996

Delicious, quite delicious. Nothing quite, however, or quiet about the fruit which is rich, ripe and full. Top 220 stores.

AUSTRALIAN WINE   WHITE

Annie's Lane Semillon, Clare Valley 1996   17   D

Absolutely hums with multi-layered flavours (peaches, plums, hint of strawberry).

Australian Dry White 1998, Safeway   14.5   B

Australian Marsanne 1997, Safeway   13.5   D

Australian Oaked Chardonnay 1998, Safeway   16   C

Wonderful plumpness and textured freshness. Superb chardonnay for under a fiver.

Australian Oaked Colombard 1998, Safeway   14   B

Basedow Semillon, Barossa Valley 1997   15   D

Wonderful fish supper treat, this wine. It manages to offer health and wealth, freshness and fruit, fullness and delicacy. Top 120 stores.

Breakaway Chenin/Sauvignon 1998   11   C

Top 280 stores.

Capel Vale Unwooded Chardonnay 1998   13   E

Top 120 stores.

Capel Vale Verdelho 1998 `15.5` `E`

Unusually rich and gently spicy – great for oriental food. Very classy. Top twenty-three stores.

Chardonnay/Colombard 1998, Safeway `15` `C`

Geoff Merrill Reserve Chardonnay 1996 `16` `E`

Real treat. Mature, vegetal, Meursault-like acidity with a coating of Aussie warmth. Top 120 stores from June.

Hardys Nottage Hill Chardonnay 1997 `16.5` `C`

Fantastic oily/buttery texture, ripe fruit, just terrific.

Lindemans Bin 65 Chardonnay 1998 `16` `C`

One of the chicest, most expressive chardonnays under a fiver out of Australia.

Lindemans Winemaker's Reserve Padthaway 1995 `13` `G`

Mount Hurtle Chardonnay 1996 `15` `D`

Oxford Landing Estate Viognier 1998 `15` `D`

Develops, from a demure start, into a lovely calm apricot-tinged, dry wine of some class. Will cellar well for three or four years. Top fifty-three stores.

Penfolds The Valleys Chardonnay 1997 `14.5` `D`

Polish Hill River Vineyard Riesling, Clare Valley 1998 `15` `E`

For riesling freaks now, for normal mortals in two years or so when the fruit will really have developed. Top 110 stores.

Riddoch Chardonnay, Coonawarra 1996

Super mouth-filling plumpness of ripe fruit here, hint of caramel cream even, but the acidity surges alongside in support and the finish is regal. Very classy wine.

Robertson Barrel Fermented Colombard 1998

Most stores.

Rosemount Estate Chardonnay 1997 (1.5 litre)

A classy beast of true pedigree feel from start to finish. Superbly chic and classy. Price bracket has been adjusted to show bottle equivalent.

Rosemount Show Reserve Chardonnay 1997

Such style and wit here. And it'll age for two or three years and grow more pointed. At most stores.

Rothbury Estate Verdelho, Hunter Valley 1998

Makes a wonderful case for the grape as a spicier version of chardonnay. Great stuff.

Taltarni Sauvignon Blanc, Victoria 1998

Dry, restrained richness, a hint of under-ripe melon. Has class. Will cellar well for two or three years. Top 110 stores.

AUSTRIAN WINE WHITE

Cat's Leap Gruner Veltliner 1997 `12.5` `C`

At most stores.

BULGARIAN WINE RED

Azbuka Merlot 1996 `12` `D`

Bit juicy for my blood – though tannins are there. Top 121 stores.

Bulgarian Country Wine, Merlot/Pinot Noir 1997, Safeway `15.5` `B`

Huntman's Red, Cabernet/Merlot 1997 `15.5` `B`

Oaked Merlot, Rousse 1997, Safeway `13.5` `C`

Vinenka Merlot/Gamza Reserve, Suhindol 1993 `14` `B`

BULGARIAN WINE WHITE

Bulgarian Chardonnay, Rousse 1998, Safeway `16` `B`

Deliciously proper and posh. Better than many a white burgundy.

Bulgarian Oaked Chardonnay 1997, Safeway

Delightful amalgam of gentle wood and firm fruit.

CHILEAN WINE   RED

35 Sur Cabernet Sauvignon, Lontue 1997

Caballo Loco No 2, Valdivieso NV

Carta Vieja Merlot 1998

Superb turn of speed as the fruit surges across the taste buds in Protean layers of richness. Most stores.

Casa Lapostolle Cuvee Alexandre Merlot, Rapel 1997

Who gives a toss for £100 Petrus when there is this rich, hugely complex beauty on sale for eleven pounds? Top 119 stores.

Castillo de Molina Cabernet Sauvignon Reserva, Lontue 1996 17 D

A stunning cabernet with piles of rich tannic fruit and cassis/ chocolate undertones. A marvellously fluent yet dry wine of massive charm, depth, complexity and lingering fruit. Selected stores.

Chilean Cabernet Sauvignon 1998, Safeway

It's not classic and peppery but it is cabernet. But cabernet as soft, rich, deep and utterly quaffably delish.

Concha y Toro Casillero del Diablo
Cabernet Sauvignon, Maipo 1997

Motors in top gear across the whole sensory system: has such gorgeous tannins!

Errazuriz Syrah Reserve, Aconcagua 1997

Big, berried fruit, rugged yet immensely soft, huge depth, flavour and commanding richness. This is even better than it was in the summer of '98 when I first tasted it.

Genesis Vineyards, Palmeras Estate Oak
Aged Cabernet Sauvignon, Nancagua 1996

Brilliance and bite here from the vigour of the fruit, dry and lingering, to the cigar-box finish. Very classy stuff. Astonishingly good value.

Isla Negra Merlot 1998

What superb dryness yet riveting rich leathery fruit! It's marvellous drinking. Top 219 stores.

Soleca Cabernet/Merlot, Colchagua 1997 15 C

TerraMater Merlot 1998 13 C

Bit juicy – tannins all in very late. Most stores from June.

TerraMater Zinfandel/Syrah, Maipo 1998 16.5 C

Superb clashing of spice and bright hedgerow fruitiness. Wonderful deep texture and tension here. Scrumptious. Top 117 stores.

Valdivieso Cabernet Franc Reserve, Lontue 1996 `16` `E`

Classier than any Chinon, that's for sure.

Valdivieso Malbec Reserve, Lontue 1996 `15.5` `E`

A soft, caressing malbec of lushness yet never soppiness. Delicious quaffing. Top 119 stores.

Valdivieso Merlot Reserve, Lontue 1997 `16.5` `E`

Accomplished winemaking here. Old leather, tannins, sweet hedgerow fruit and a lush yet dry finish. Lovely wine. At most stores.

Villard Vineyards Cabernet Sauvignon, Maipo 1996 `16.5` `D`

Why is this wine so good? Let me tell you. It has texture (soft) plus character (raunchy) and such well-knitted tannins to the ripe fruit. Selected stores.

Vina Morande Merlot 1998 `17` `C`

This has fruit so textured and rich it surprises like fluid grease. Incredible leathery lushness here.

CHILEAN WINE WHITE

35 Sur Sauvignon Blanc 1998 `16`

Superb! The grassiness of the acidity and the richness of fruit, still classic dry sauvignon, make for a wonderful crisp mouthful. Selected stores.

Casa Lapostolle Cuvee Alexandre
Chardonnay, Casablanca 1996   17.5   E

One of the best chardonnays in the world. Simply gorgeous texture, complex fruit and sheer charm. Top twenty-nine stores only.

Castillo de Molina Reserva Semillon,
Lontue 1997   14   D

Chilean Sauvignon Blanc Lontue 1998,
Safeway   16   C

Combining great nuttiness and gooseberry, nettle-fresh fruit. Huge charm and subtle richness.

Chilean Semillon/Chardonnay 1998,
Safeway   16   C

Baked fruit mixed with fresh. Wonderful stuff!

Chilean White, Lontue 1998, Safeway   16   B

What a price for such depth, elegance, freshness and flavour.

Cordillera Estate Oak Aged Chardonnay
Reserva 1997, Safeway   15.5   C

Soleca Semillon/Chardonnay, Colchagua
1997   16   C

Clever winemaking here. Modern wizardry creating class, richness and style.

TerraMater Chardonnay, Maipo 1997   16   C

Astonishing richness yet charm (of relaxed manners) here. Selected stores.

**Vina Gracia Chardonnay 'Reposado',
Cachapoal 1997** `14` `C`

ENGLISH WINE WHITE

**Stanlake, Thames Valley Vineyards 1996,
Safeway** `13.5` `C`

FRENCH WINE RED

Beaune 1996, Safeway `10` `E`

**Bergerie de l'Arbous Domaine Jean Jean,
Eleve en Futs de Chene 1996** `14` `D`

Dry yet juicy. Not as compelling as previous vintages of this wine. Top 220 stores.

Bordeaux Merlot 1998 `13` `C`

Bit austere. At most stores.

**Chateau Barde-Haut, St Emilion Grand
Cru 1995** `13` `F`

Yes, it's an odd vintage and it shows how ill-knitted together it is in spite of some fine rich-edged tannicity. But the price . . .

Chateau de Cordes, Minervois 1997 `14.5` `C`

Starts ripe, goes all coy and half-hearted, then opens up with some lovely touches. Top 220 stores.

Chateau du Grison, Bordeaux 1995 `12.5` `D`

Chateau du Piras, Premieres Cotes de Bordeaux 1994 `14` `D`

Chateau Maison Neuve Montagne St Emilion 1996 `15` `E`

Gets a bit rugged and crotchety on the finish but the tannins and leathery fruit are in rip-roaring form. Very, very classy, dry and rich and firmly concentrated. Very clarety.

Chateau Soudars, Cru Bourgeois 1994 `14` `E`

Corbieres 1998, Safeway `16` `B`

What a fleshily fruity, very civilised bargain. Herbs, sun, gentle tannins and real style.

Cotes du Rhone Oak Aged 1997, Safeway `12` `C`

Crozes-Hermitage, Domaine Barret 1997 `13` `D`

Close to being rather good, but the price demands we must take it seriously. The fruit is soft and plump, with some earthy character, but it seems to be perfunctory on the finish.

Domaine Chris Limouzi, Eleve en Futs de Chene Corbieres 1997 `16` `D`

Ripe yet dry, cosy yet argumentative, this is a hugely approachable wine of great class. Top 220 stores.

Domaine de Boriettes Syrah, VdP
d'Oc 1998

Very fresh and dry on the finish but the tannins are active and flowing.

Domaine de Condamine, Fitou 1997
13 C

Bit too ripe and juicy on the finish. Top 220 stores.

Domaine de Tudery Saint Chinian 1997
14 D

Finishes strongly, from a juicy start. Top 219 stores.

Domaine des Bruyeres, Cotes de Malepere
1998
16.5 C

What effrontery to be so rich and complex, dry and decisive, for such a small sum of money. It's a lovely wine.

Domaine des Lauriers, Faugeres 1996

Superb texture here. It resounds with aromatic and fruity hints of the Midi scrub and hedgerows, orchards and earth. Wonderful tannins. Top 220 stores.

Domaine Vieux Manoir de Maransan Cuvee
Speciale 1997, Safeway
15 C

Gevrey Chambertin Domaine Rossignol-
Trapet 1996

Intensely dull for the money. Well, it would be dull at £2.99. Does it try? A bit. But its outlandish price makes enthusiasm impossible.

Graves Cuvee Prestige 1994
13 D

**Hautes Cotes de Nuits Cuvee Speciale
1995** 12 E

L'If Merlot/Carignan, VdP du Torgan 1998 14 C

Intensely dry and firmly tannic. Will soften beautifully over
the year.

**'La Source de Mirail' Grenache/Syrah, VdP
de Vaucluse 1997** 15 B

La Source Merlot/Syrah VdP d'Oc 1998 15.5 C

Herbs and rocks, hillside scrub and well cooked fruit. Finishes
dry yet very satisfyingly.

Le Haut-Medoc de Giscours 1995 13.5 E

**Les Hauts de Montauriol, Cotes du
Frontonnais 1996** 15.5 C

March Hare VdP d'Oc 1998 13.5 C

Mercurey Raoul Clerget 1996 12 E

Merlot Selection 24 VdP d'Oc 1998 15.5 C

Very faintly leathery tannins and fresh herbs coat the fruit.
Impressive. Top 219 stores.

Minervois 1998, Safeway 15 B

Terrific herby, dry yet textured richness.

Oak-aged Medoc 1996, Safeway 13.5 D

Organic French Red VdP du Gard NV, Safeway `14` `C`

Pommard 1er Cru 'Les Clos des Boucherottes' 1996 `10` `G`

Richemont Montbrun Old Vine Carignan VdP de l'Aude 1995 `14` `D`

Richemont Reserve Merlot, VdP d'Oc 1996 `14` `C`

Saint-Joseph 'Cuvee Cote-Diane' 1995 `14` `E`

Savigny du Domaine du Chateau de Meursault 1996 `11` `E`

St Emilion 1996 `13.5` `D`

Syrah VdP d'Oc 1998, Safeway `14.5` `B`

Juicy fruits yet wry and dry on the finish.

Winter Hill Merlot/Grenache, VdP d'Oc 1998 `15` `B`

Very dry and richly characterful. Not a pussycat at all. But it still purrs. At most stores.

FRENCH WINE   WHITE

Bordeaux Blanc Sec Aged in Oak 1997, Safeway `13` `C`

169

Bordeaux Sauvignon, Calvet 1997 `12` `C`

Chablis Premier Cru Montmains 1997 `10` `F`

Chateau du Plantier Entre Deux Mers 1997 `13` `C`

Chateau du Roc Bordeaux Sauvignon 1998 `10` `C`

The specimen I tried tasted 'of old peapods' according to one Safeway wine buyer.

Chateau Magneau, Graves 1997 `14` `D`

Cotes du Luberon Rose 1997, Safeway `14` `C`

Domaine du Rey, VdP des Cotes de Gascogne 1997 (vegetarian) `13.5` `C`

En Sol Kimmeridgien, Bourgogne Blanc 1997 `11` `D`

Pretty dull for seven quid. Top 280 stores.

Gewurztraminer d'Alsace 1997, Safeway `16.5` `D`

Stunning smoky fruit redolent of gently spicy crushed rose petals. Captivatingly fruity.

L'If Grenache Blanc, VdP du Torgan 1998 `16.5` `C`

What a wonderfully rich and refreshing change from chardonnay! It's a triumph of layered complexity.

La Baume Sauvignon Blanc, VdP d'Oc 1997 `14` `C`

La Loustere VdP du Gers 1998　　14.5　B

Lovely gentle exotic undertone for summer. At most stores.

La Source Chardonnay/Roussanne VdP d'Oc 1998　　14　C

Soft and hinting at nuttiness.

Pinot Blanc Alsace 1998, Safeway　　13.5　C

Needs a six month lie-down to knit its ragged edges together. Will be fine for Christmas smoked salmon.

Rochemartain Sauvignon Touraine 1997　　14　C

Sancerre 'Les Bonnes Bouches' Domaine Henri Bourgeois 1997　　12.5　E

Sauvignon Blanc Cuvee Reserve VdP d'Oc 1998　　16　C

Lovely dry nuttiness and a crisp, decisive edge. Sullen richness here, good in a sauvignon, makes it a classic. Top 280 stores.

Wild Trout VdP d'Oc 1998　　15.5　C

Dignified and dainty, rich yet controlled. Outstanding blend of tasty grapes.

GERMAN WINE　　WHITE

Fire Mountain Riesling, Pfalz 1996　　13.5　C

**Hattenheimer Heiligenberg Riesling
Kabinett, Rheingau 1996** `13` `D`

Kenderman Dry Riesling, Pfalz 1997 `13` `C`

**Oppenheimer Sacktrager Riesling
Kabinett, Rheinhessen 1996** `12` `D`

**Pudding Wine, Pfalz Auslese NV (half
bottle)** `15` `C`

Riesling Classic, Pfalz 1996 `15` `B`

**Rupertsberger Nussbein Riesling Kabinett
1995** `14` `C`

Still young and searching for its soul (mineralised acidity like
licking a slate tile). But it's still got some crisp class to it – but
wait five or six years . . .

**Scharzhofberger Riesling Spatlese,
Mosel-Saar-Ruwer 1996** `16` `E`

Gorgeous! And what a stylish aperitif it makes. Top sixty-four
stores.

**Weinheimer Sybillenstein Beerenauslese,
Rheinhessen 1993 (half bottle)** `16` `D`

Superb, honeyed, nutty, sweet wine with rampant fruitiness and
compatibility with fresh fruit and desserts. Selected stores.

GREEK WINE RED

Mavrodaphne of Patras NV `14.5` `C`

HUNGARIAN WINE   RED

Bull's Blood 1997   13   B

**Hungarian Cabernet Sauvignon, Villany
1996**   15.5 C

River Duna Kekfrancos, Szekszard 1997   14.5 B

HUNGARIAN WINE   WHITE

**Chapel Hill Barrique-fermented
Chardonnay 1996, Safeway**   15   C

Hilltop Bianca 1998 (organic)   15.5 B

Superbly textured and richly polished organic wine of great
integral freshness yet fruitiness. At most stores from mid-July.

**Hungarian Chardonnay, Buda 1997,
Safeway**   13.5 B

**Hungarian Dry Muscat Nagyrede 1997,
Safeway**   14   B

**Hungarian Irsai Oliver, Neszmely 1998,
Safeway**   15   B

Compelling aperitif. Daintily floral fruit. Terrific picnic wine.

**Matra Mountain Oaked Chardonnay,
Nagyrede 1998, Safeway**

**Matra Mountain Sauvignon Blanc 1998,
Safeway**

At most stores.

Nagyrede Oaked Zenit 1998

Riverview Chardonnay 1997

Soft and bruisedly fruity. Not subtle. At most stores.

Riverview Gewurztraminer 1997

In the top fifty-five stores from mid-July.

Woodcutter's White, Neszmely 1998

Doesn't develop a gripping finish but it gets there deliciously
fruitily and charmingly.

ITALIAN WINE
RED

Alto Varo Rosso di Puglia 1997

Sweet and dry contrast – ends dryly. Needs pasta (with bacon
bits).

Amarone delle Valpolicella Classico 1993

Uniquely cherry/plum/blackberry dry, rich wine with a hint of
marzipan. Wonderful fruit here.

Chianti 1997, Safeway `14` `C`

Di Giorno Merlot/Corvina, Veneto 1997 `13.5` `B`

Mimosa Maremma Sangiovese 1997 `16` `C`

Fantastically earthy-edged, rich, deep, dry, clotted and captivatingly fruity wine of great charm. An outstanding barbecued-meat wine. Top 289 stores.

Salice Salento Riserva 1994 `14` `D`

Serina Primitivo, Tarantino, Puglia 1996 `15` `C`

A gutsy red with weight and wit – odd dry plum finish – a hint if not an echo of spice – but a welcoming brew of a bottle on a cool evening.

Sicilian Red 1997, Safeway `12` `B`

Valpolicella Valpatena 'Corte Alta' 1997 `14` `C`

ITALIAN WINE   WHITE

**Casa di Giovanni Grillo 1997, Safeway
(Sicily)** `16` `C`

Utterly gorgeous fruit! Terrific opulence and gently toasty lemon.

**Chardonnay del Salento Barrique-aged,
Caramia 1996** `15` `D`

Marc Xero Chardonnay, Salento 1997 `13` `C`

Has a screwcap! Delicious innovation. The fruit is somewhat less innovative. Coming into the top 235 stores from mid-June.

Sicilian White 1997, Safeway `14.5` `B`

Tenuta 'Pietra Porzia' Frascati Superiore 1997 `15` `C`

MEXICAN WINE RED

L A Cetto Malbec 1997 `15.5` `C`

MONTENEGRAN WINE RED

Monte Cheval Vranac 1993 `13.5` `C`

NEW ZEALAND WINE RED

Church Road Cabernet Sauvignon/Merlot 1996 `14` `E`

Still green and austere by the standards of European orchards (Bordeaux excepted), this has some peppery class to make up for the vegetality.

**Delegat's Reserve Cabernet Sauvignon
Barrique Matured 1997** `14` `E`

Lot of money. Top fourteen stores from mid-June.

Ninth Island Pinot Noir, Tasmania 1998 `13` `E`

Top forty stores.

NEW ZEALAND WINE WHITE

**Delegat's Reserve Chardonnay, Barrel
Fermented 1997** `13.5` `E`

Very chewy and ungainly woody. Top fifty-three stores.

**Goldwater 'Dog Point' Sauvignon Blanc
1998** `14` `E`

Dainty, possessing poise and finesse, expensive, dry. Top fifty-three stores.

**Ninth Island Sauvignon Blanc, Tasmania
1998** `13.5` `E`

Four quid wine. Top fifty-three stores.

Oyster Bay Chardonnay, Marlborough 1998 `16.5` `D`

Superb creamy, gently smoky fruit. It is a very classy performer. Top 120 stores.

**Oyster Bay Sauvignon Blanc, Marlborough
1998** `16` `D`

Dry honey edges to the warm gooseberry-fool fruit, and a fresh finish. Selected stores.

Villa Maria Private Bin Chardonnay 1998 | 14 | D |

Needs a year to deliver its closed complexity. Top 235 stores.

Villa Maria Private Bin Sauvignon Blanc, Marlborough 1998 | 17 | D |

Elegant and chic, beautifully designed. The tongue rarely wears such perfectly fitted fruit.

Villa Maria Reserve Wairau Valley Sauvignon 1998 | 15.5 | E |

Keep it for eighteen months. Sure, it's lovely and elegant now but it will richly develop in bottle and possibly rate 17/18 points in a couple of years. Top fifty-three stores.

PORTUGUESE WINE   RED

Bela Fonte Baga 1997 | 15.5 | C |

Terrific juicy fruit here. Delicious tarry richness and mature juiciness.

Falua, Ribetajo 1998, Safeway | 14 | B |

Dry, hint of earth, cherries well baked. Most stores.

Miradouro Portuguese Red, Terras do Sado 1996 | 13 | B |

Sinfonia, Alentejo 1997 | 16.5 | C |

The sheer polish of this wine is taste-bud-tinglingly rich and well textured. Superb fruit of great class for the money.

Vila Regia Douro 1995

ROMANIAN WINE RED

Pinot Noir Special Reserve 1995, Safeway 14.5 C

SOUTH AFRICAN WINE RED

**Bouwland Cabernet Sauvignon/Merlot,
Stellenbosch 1997** 14 D

Gobbets of rich earth and ripe fruit. Top 210 stores.

Delaire Cabernet Sauvignon Merlot 1997 15 E

Expensive treat. Has edges of tobacco and cassis, rather ripely
in cahoots, and a finish of soft leather and baked plums.
Not a classicist's cabernet but superbly gluggable. Top fourteen stores.

Fairview Pinotage 1998 16.5 D

Utterly compulsive glugging here: rich, smoky, beautifully inter-
twined spicy fruit and tannins. Wonderful! Top 292 stores.

**Kanonkop Cabernet Sauvignon,
Stellenbosch 1994** 13.5 F

**Kanonkop 'Kadette' Estate Wine,
Stellenbosch 1996** 14 D

Kleinbosch Young Vatted Pinotage, Paarl 1998 `16` `C`

So vibrant and perky it shakes one's teeth to their roots! Lovely ripe fruit here.

Kleindal Pinotage 1997, Safeway `15` `C`

Landskroon Cinsaut/Shiraz, Paarl 1998 `16` `C`

What an improvement on the '97! This is jammy, spicy and soft (yet fresh) but with good tannins. A masterly food wine.

Plaisir de Merle Cabernet Sauvignon, Paarl 1995 `15` `F`

Plantation Ruby Cabernet, Stellenbosch 1998 `15.5` `C`

Simonsvlei Shiraz Reserve 1998 `14` `C`

Highly aromatic and well charged with vibrant fruit. Top 140 stores.

Stellenbosch Cabernet Sauvignon 1998 `C`

Welcoming, full yet dry, textured, ripe, real tannic blackcurrants. Classy. Most stores.

Stellenbosch Merlot 1997 `C`

The Pinotage Company Selected Bush Vine Pinotage 1998 `16` `D`

Tasted the morning after Bill Clinton's televised squirmings, I found this wine fruitier by far.

SOUTH AFRICAN WINE   WHITE

Arniston Bay Chenin Chardonnay 1998

Extremely forward but not flashy. Has warmth and piles of soft fruit but manages to stay refreshing and engagingly plump without being obscenely Rubenesque.

Bouchard Finlayson Oak Valley Chardonnay 1996

Rich, smoky, very fat on the finish, and chewily woody. Only at the top nine stores.

Brampton Sauvignon Blanc 1997

Chenin Blanc Stellenbosch, Safeway 1998

Delaire Chardonnay, Stellenbosch 1997

Toasted nuts, hint of gunsmoke, tight gooseberry and melon fruit, gently viscous texture, terrific finish. A very convincing wine.

Fairview Estate Semillon, Paarl 1997

Wonderfully concentrated and freshly turned out. Has great lingering dry peach, vanillary and icy mineral undertones all packed together stylishly and sagely. Utterly delicious wine of class and composure.

Kleinezalze Sauvignon Blanc 1997

Namaqua Colombard, Olifantsrivier 1998

Plantation Semillon 1998

Gorgeous concentrated gooseberry juiced wine with a further fruity layer, subtle, of lime. Utterly delicious – quenching and thought provocative.

Robertson Barrel Fermented Chardonnay 1997

Chardonnay in the new-world, sub-citrus, gently woody style where the fruit is freshly picked, never cloying or taut, but just giving, clean and delicious.

South African Chardonnay 1998, Safeway

Swartland Reserve Bush Vine Chenin Blanc 1998

Has a heart of steely-crisp fruit, a hint of gooseberries, a touch of cos lettuce and a suspicion of nut. Complex goings on for four quid.

Vergelegen Chardonnay, Stellenbosch 1997

Very lemonic and fresh. Not complex. Top fifty-one stores.

SPANISH WINE RED

Bach Merlot, Penedes 1996

Beware! Tannin attack! Oh what heaven! The squeamish are warned! Selected stores.

Berberana Tempranillo Rioja, 1996   14   C

Cosme Palacio y Hermanos Rioja 1996   14.5   D

El Leon Mencia, Bierzo 1997   14   C

El Velero Monastrell, Murcia 1997   12   B

Marques de Murrieta, Rioja Reserva 1993   13.5   E

**Marques de Riscal Rioja Gran Reserva
1989**   16   G

A point for every penny it costs. The acme of old style, vanilla
rich, tannic Rioja. Fabulous stuff. Top thirty-three stores.

Muruve Toro 1997   15.5   C

**Santara Cabernet/Merlot, Conca de
Barbera 1996**   16.5   C

One of the great under-a-fiver reds of supermarketing and Spain.
Rich, mature, claret-like aroma, big, dry, cassis-edged fruit with
a hint of chocolate and tobacco and a roaring, handsomely
dishevelled finish. A smooth rough diamond of deliciousness.

**Young Vatted Tempranillo, La Mancha
1997, Safeway**   14   B

SPANISH WINE   WHITE

**CVNE Monopole Barrel-fermented
Rioja 1995**   12   D

183

El Velero Dry White, Valdepenas 1997

El Velero Rosé, Valdepenas 1998

Superb summer rosé: rich, plump and dryly fruity. Great with all sorts of food. At most stores.

USA WINE RED

Dunnewood Zinfandel, Barrel Select 1994

Fetzer Barrel Select Cabernet Sauvignon 1994

Great opulence and richness here. Coats the teeth like emulsion. Has bite and backbone.

Kenwood Lodi Old Vine Zinfandel 1996

Touch overbaked and soupy. Top forty stores.

USA WINE WHITE

Californian Oak-aged Chardonnay 1997, Safeway

Dunnewood California Chardonnay 1996

Gorgeous texture and great litheness with the balance of wood and fruit in perfect harmony. A hugely impressive Californian chardonnay without being attached to an obscene price tag.

Fetzer Chardonnay Reserve 1995 | 16 | F |

Did white burgundy, Montrachet say, ever taste this good in the good old days? Nope, never. This is a white wine of great class, richness, balance, and sheer world-class finish.

Fetzer Echo Ridge Sauvignon Blanc 1997 | 15.5 | C |

If Pouilly Fume tasted like this, it'd cost twenty quid a bottle.

Fetzer Viognier 1997 | 16 | E |

Exuberant, spicy, richly elegant yet expressive of fun and roses, with gooseberries and apricots, this is a deliciously swirling, all-dancing viognier of great charm.

Ironstone Chardonnay 1997 | 15.5 | D |

Lovely rich fruit, polished and buttery, and with great litheness. It's a muscular yet very spry wine of depth and decisiveness. Very good price.

FORTIFIED WINE

10 Year Old Tawny Port, Safeway | 14.5 | F |

Amontillado, Safeway | 13 | C |

Barbadillo Solear Manzanilla | 14 | D |

Dow's 20-year old Tawny | 16 | H |

What a price! What a wine! To be drunk the night before the morning you get taken out and shot.

Fino, Safeway `14` `C`

Fonseca Guimaraens 1982 `13` `G`

Penfolds Magill Tawny (half bottle) `14` `D`

Warre's Traditional LBV 1984 `14.5` `G`

Warre's Vintage Port, Quinta da Cavadinha 1986 `17` `G`

A most unusually complete port where alcohol, sugar, acid and tannin meld in mouth-watering harmony.

Warre's Warrior Finest Reserva `14` `E`

SPARKLING WINE/CHAMPAGNE

Albert Etienne Champagne Vintage 1993, Safeway `13` `G`

Charles Heidsieck 'Mis en Cave 1994' Champagne `13` `H`

Chenin Brut, Vin Mousseux de Qualite (France) `14` `C`

Conde de Caralt Cava Brut NV `16.5` `D`

As elegant a cava as they come. Knocks a thousand Champagnes into oblivion. Top 280 stores from mid-June.

Cuvee Signe Champagne, Nicholas Feuillate NV `14.5` `G`

Undeniably possessed of great haughty finesse and class. Top 235 stores.

Graham Beck Brut NV (South Africa) `14` `D`

Crisp and gently fruity.

Lanson Champagne Demi-Sec Ivory Label NV `12` `G`

Bit too brutal for the classicist and the price sucks.

Lindauer Brut NV (New Zealand) `14.5` `E`

Expressive of nothing but great value for money and utterly charming sipping.

Louis Roederer Champagne Brut Premier NV `13` `H`

Top fifty-three stores.

Merlot/Gamay Brut NV (France) `16` `C`

Yes, a red vin mousseux! And with summer barbecues it's brilliant. Pert, fruity, not remotely eccentric. Lovely style here. At most stores.

Nicholas Feuillate Champagne Blanc de Blancs NV `14` `G`

Piper-Heidsieck Champagne Vintage 1990 `13` `H`

Yes, it has charm. But twenty-three quid's worth? Nope. Top 235 stores.

187

Pol Acker Chardonnay Brut (France) `14` `C`

Pommery Brut Royal Champagne NV `12` `H`

Absurd price and fruit. Top fifty-three stores from mid-June.

Seaview Pinot Noir/Chardonnay 1995 (Australia) `16` `E`

Gorgeous, elegant stuff. Real class here.

Segura Viudas Cava Brut 1994 `13` `E`

Selection XXI, Champagne, Nicholas Feuillate NV `13` `G`

At most stores.

Veuve Clicquot Champagne Vintage Reserve 1991 `14` `H`

A rare treat. A fabulously priced Champagne which shows its class. Top fifty-three stores.

Veuve Clicquot Champagne Yellow Label Brut NV `11` `H`

Safeway plc
Safeway House
6 Millington Road
Hayes UB3 4AY
Tel 0181 848 8744
Fax 0181 573 1865

SAINSBURY'S

ARGENTINIAN WINE   RED

Mendoza Cabernet Sauvignon/Malbec NV, Sainsbury's

Textured, tauntingly rich and ripe, dry and deep. Great food wine.

Mendoza Country Red NV, Sainsbury's

Superb value for money: a sticky, rich yet accomplished and well-balanced fruity specimen of great charm.

ARGENTINIAN WINE   WHITE

Mendoza Country White NV, Sainsbury's

Fantastic value: real rich, balanced, clean fruit.

Tupungato Chardonnay Chenin NV, Sainsbury's

Selected stores.

AUSTRALIAN WINE   RED

Australian Cabernet Sauvignon, Sainsbury's

Australian Red Wine NV, Sainsbury's (3-litre box)

`15` `B`

Price bracket has been adjusted to the 75cl equivalent.

Clancy's Shiraz/Cabernet Sauvignon/ Merlot/Cabernet Franc 1996

`15` `E`

Hardys Cabernet Shiraz Merlot 1995

`14.5` `D`

Selected stores.

Hardys Stamp Series Shiraz Cabernet Sauvignon 1997

`14` `C`

Leasingham Cabernet Sauvignon Malbec 1996

`14.5` `E`

Leasingham Domaine Shiraz 1996

`15` `E`

Some character and rich fruit here. Soupy yes, but there is a hint of backbone to the flesh. Seventy stores.

Lindemans Padthaway Pinot Noir 1997

`15` `E`

McPhersons Shiraz 1997

`16` `C`

More like Aussie reds should be – soft, cheap, rich, dry, biting. food-friendly, characterful. Forty-four stores.

Mount Hurtle Cabernet Merlot 1996

`14` `D`

Penfolds Bin 389 Cabernet Shiraz 1995

`15` `F`

Expensive muscle here. It's a bouncer of a wine: you don't get in without a hassle. Highly drinkable with food – spicy, rich, deep. Eighty stores.

Rosemount Diamond Label Shiraz 1997

Rosemount Estate Shiraz Cabernet 1998

So deliciously sweet and fruity: soft and full yet delicate on the finish. Deliciously approachable and warm.

Saltram Classic Cabernet Sauvignon 1996

Saltram Classic Shiraz 1996

**Stowells Australian Red Mataro/Shiraz NV
(3-litre box)**

Price bracket has been adjusted to the 75cl equivalent.

**Tarrawingee Mourvedre Shiraz NV,
Sainsbury's**

So ripe it takes the enamel off your teeth! Great casserole wine. Selected stores.

Tyrrells Old Winery Cabernet Merlot 1997

115 stores.

**Wolf Blass Yellow Label Cabernet
Sauvignon 1997** `16` `E`

Fabulous rich fruit which would be wonderful with Indian food. Ripe and rampant. Selected stores.

Wynns Coonawarra Shiraz 1996 `16.5` `D`

Superbly classy and rich. Hints of mint cling to the deeply

textured (denim and corduroy) fruit (plums, cherries and black-currants) and the sheer cheek of the fruit, its bounce yet gravitas, is terrific – the finish is syrup of figs.

AUSTRALIAN WINE WHITE

Australian Chardonnay NV, Sainsbury's

Superb value for money. Great richness and acidic balance here. Remarkable value.

Australian Semillon Chardonnay NV, Sainsbury's (3-litre box)

Price bracket has been adjusted to the 75cl equivalent.

Australian Semillon Sauvignon Blanc, Sainsbury's

Delicious texture, gently oily and rich, lots of rich vegetal hints (unusual in an Aussie white), and a dry, hint-of-nut finish. Selected stores.

Australian White Wine NV, Sainsbury's (3-litre box)

Price bracket has been adjusted to the 75cl equivalent.

Bridgewater Mill Chardonnay, South Australia 1996

Delicious creamy/smoky ripeness yet elegance. Comes across like

194

a Californian so it's warm without being sweaty, a touch vegetal (white burgundian), yet beautifully textured and balanced. Ninety-five stores.

Hardys Banrock Station Chenin Blanc/Semillon/Chardonnay 1997

Shows the real elegance of the '97 Aussie whites.

Hardys Chardonnay Sauvignon Blanc 1997

A rich sauvignon with hints of vegetality and dry gooseberry richness. Great food wine. 130 stores.

Jacobs Creek Semillon/Chardonnay 1998

Old warhorse still good value and richly fruity (but balanced).

Lindemans Bin 65 Chardonnay 1998 16 C

Supremely sure of itself, this well-established brand showing, in its '98 manifestation, what a great year this is for Aussie whites from the region (Hunter Valley). This has great hints of warm fruit balanced by complex crispness and acidity. A lovely under-a-fiver bobby dazzler.

Lindemans Cawarra Homestead Unoaked Chardonnay 1998 14 C

Lovely rich edge to the fresh, never over-baked fruit.

Lindemans Padthaway Chardonnay 1996

Penfolds Rawsons Retreat Bin 21 Semillon/Chardonnay/Colombard 1997

Penfolds The Valleys Chardonnay 1997 `14.5` `E`

Rosemount Estate Diamond Label Chardonnay 1997 `16` `D`

One of the great island's classiest chardonnays – here showing the forwardness of the brilliant '97 vintage.

Rosemount Show Reserve Chardonnay 1997 `16` `E`

Hugely elegant treat wine with classic richness, vegetality, finesse and masses of real depth of charm. Eighty-five stores.

Saltram Classic Chardonnay 1997 `16` `C`

Has a wonderful melon richness with lemon/pineapple edging. 140 stores.

Tyrrells Old Winery Chardonnay 1997 `12` `D`

Selected stores.

Wynns Coonawarra Estate Chardonnay 1996 `16.5` `E`

Most delightful chardonnay with a lingering depth of flavour like gently toffeed melon. Zippy fun. Ninety stores.

Wynns Coonawarra Riesling 1996 `15` `C`

BULGARIAN WINE RED

Bulgarian Cabernet Sauvignon, Sainsbury's (3-litre box) `13.5` `C`

Price bracket has been adjusted to the 75cl equivalent.

Bulgarian Country Dry Red, Russe, Sainsbury's (1.5 litre) `14.5` **B**

Price bracket has been adjusted to the 75cl equivalent.

Bulgarian Reserve Merlot, Suhindol 1994 `13.5` **C**

Czar Simeon Bulgarian Cabernet Sauvignon 1990 `13.5` **D**

Domaine Boyar Cabernet Sauvignon Reserve 1994 `13` **C**

Very juicy.

Domaine Boyar Premium Oak Barrel Aged Merlot 1997 `14` **C**

Sweet but very dry. Good for curries and what not.

JS Bulgarian Merlot, Oak Aged, Russe `13.5` **B**

Vintage Blend Oriachovitza Merlot & Cabernet Sauvignon Reserve 1994 `16` **C**

Very ripe and mature yet still in its prime fruitwise as it finishes: dry, plum and blackcurranty, with a hint of thick tannin. Lovely stuff. Not at all stores.

CHILEAN WINE   RED

35 Sur Cabernet Sauvignon 1998 `16.5` **C**

Superb cabernet of wit, warmth, character, concentration, softness yet dryness, approachability yet seriousness and a great potency of flavour on the finish. A vivacious cabernet of punch and pertinacity.

Chilean Cabernet Sauvignon/Merlot NV, Sainsbury's   16   C

Volatile on the nostrils and slightly overripe but the fruit is brilliant: dry, rich, flavourful and character packed. Real class runs through it. Wonderful rich, dry, textured stuff. Also available in a 3-litre box.

Chilean Merlot, Sainsbury's   16.5   C

Wonderful richness of tone, texture, and even a touch of soulfulness. A gorgeous, savoury, smooth wine of lingering depth.

Chilean Red, Sainsbury's   13   C

La Palma Merlot Gran Reserva 1997   17   E

Stunning aplomb here. Delivers its speech like Gielgud reading the back of a bus-ticket: fruity, soaring, arrogant, a touch disdainful, utterly and richly riveting. 100 stores.

La Palma Reserve Cabernet/Merlot 1997   16.5   D

Stunning richness and ripeness combines superbly savoury tannins and leathery soft – oh, so soft! – fruit. Selected stores.

Mont Gras Cabernet Sauvignon Reserva 1997   16.5   D

It descends by devious means. The first step is sheer fruity fun then it gets deeper, dryer and richer and finally the echo is sheer classic cabernet. Around 100 stores.

Mont Gras Carmenere Reserva 1997   13   D

Juice. 100 stores.

Mont Gras Merlot Reserva 1997

Very juicy. 105 stores.

Valdivieso Malbec 1998

Dry yet jammy, soft yet hard-edged, giving, yet has a complexity requiring an investigative nose. Selected stores.

Valdivieso Merlot, Lontue 1998

More perfumed than previous vintages and with more chewy richness on the finish.

Valdivieso Pinot Noir 1997

Keep it for a year and it'll seem like an eccentric Volnay of a sunny year. 131 stores.

Valdivieso Reserve Cabernet Sauvignon 1997

Has the lot (except an obscene price tag). But the fruit is forbidden and x-certificate: dark, dry, mysterious, touch spicy, highly aromatic and heady and finally it's so damned delicious. Hellish good drinking here. 185 stores.

Villa Montes Gran Reserva Cabernet Sauvignon 1995

Highly polished, almost luxuriously soft and ripe, aromatic, gently leathery and hugely approachable. It has a little pepperiness and supple tannicity. It is utterly at its drinkable peak.

Vina San Pedro Cabo de Hornos 1995

It pours out from the bottle in a flood of dark crimson

glints. It impinges on the nose as tobacco-scented, faintly ripe, subtly-spiced plum with a touch of leather. The fruit is controlled, rich, leathery, chocolate touches, cassis – plus tannins, ripe yet firm and in perfect alliance with the acidity and the gently vegetal, oily fruit which can be glucoid, rich and flowing because the overall sense of the wine is of dry but rich fruit. The texture? The finest ruffled velvet. Elegant, haughty, polished – it is ineffably Chilean. It has warmth in its blood, strength in its sinews, a pulse, a heart, and a soul. Etc.

CHILEAN WINE   WHITE

35 Sur Sauvignon Blanc 1998   16   C

Superb! The grassiness of the acidity and the richness of fruit, still classic dry sauvignon, makes for a wonderful crisp mouthful. Selected stores.

Chilean Chardonnay NV, Sainsbury's   15   C

Touch of grass, almond, spinach and rich melon fruit. Motley crew but great with food.

Chilean Sauvignon Blanc, Sainsbury's   15.5   C

Beautiful balance and fruity attack. Rivetingly crisp, fresh, modish fruit.

Chilean Semillon Sauvignon NV,
Sainsbury's (3-litre box)   13.5   B

Price bracket has been adjusted to the 75cl equivalent.

La Palma Chardonnay Gran Reserva 1997

Richness of fruit, yes. Finishes with a bit of a tuneless wallop. Selected stores.

Santa Carolina Chardonnay 1998

Not as rich as the '97 but has a lovely nuttiness on the finish. Selected stores.

Santa Carolina Chardonnay Reservado 1997

Smoky, creamy richness which gathers pace and lingers. Wonderful rich fish dish wine. 110 stores.

Stowells Chilean Sauvignon Blanc NV (3-litre box)

Almost good enough, but not quite. Price bracket is the 75cl equivalent.

ENGLISH WINE WHITE

Denbies Estate English table Wine NV

Duller than watching paint dry. Like chewing on a sweater. Selected stores.

Lamberhurst Sovereign Medium Dry NV

The worst label on Sainsbury's shelves fronting an ineffably boring wine.

FRENCH WINE
RED

Abbotts Cumulus Shiraz 1997
 15.5 C

The impressive fruit of the '96 is not quite so powerfully in evidence in the '97. Abbotts is herby, rich, dry and characterful and with a deft balance of elements providing class and substance. This is more playful and soft than the '96. 190 stores.

Beaujolais NV, Sainsbury's
 13.5 C

Simple glugging pleasure.

Bordeaux Rouge, Sainsbury's
 13 B

Bourgogne Pinot Noir, Boisset 1996
 12.5 D

Cabernet Sauvignon d'Oc NV, Sainsbury's
 15.5 C

Cabernet Sauvignon VdP d'Oc, Caroline Beaulieu 1997
 17 C

Superb, tobacco-edged richness, ripeness and depth and a tannic-edged finish. Fantastic class for the money.

Cahors, Sainsbury's
 13.5 C

Chartreuse de la Garde, Pessac-Leognan 1995
 15 E

Chateau Agram, Corbieres 1996
 13 C

Chateau Barreyres, Haut-Medoc 1996

Chateau Carsin, Premieres Cotes de Bordeaux 1996

Magnificent texture, ripeness, with an initial perfume of great charm, an immediate lushness which then turns seriously oily and fat in the mouth buttressed by perfectly precise tannins. A fabulous modern claret of superb depth and elegance. 150 stores.

Chateau Clement-Pichon, Haut-Medoc 1995

Chateau de Chamirey Rouge, Mercurey 1996

Selected stores.

Chateau de Gaillat, Graves 1994

Selected stores.

Chateau de la Tour Bordeaux Rouge 1996

Chateau de Lunes, Coteaux du Languedoc 1996

Chateau de Mercey, Mercurey Rouge 1995

Eighty stores.

Chateau Gloria, St Julien 1993 16.95 G

It rates a point for every penny it costs. This unique rating is deservedly attached to this glorious bottle of classic claret because of its meaty fruitiness, beautiful tannic structure, and gorgeous rich deep finish. Seventy-six stores only.

Chateau Haut Bergey, Pessac Leognan 1995

Staggeringly good texture, fronted by lush aroma and rich almost ripe blackcurrant concentration. A superb, classy Graves. Sixty stores.

Chateau Haut de la Pierriere Cotes de Castillon 1997

The essence of what minor league but bonny claret is all about: cigar boxes, bell pepper, spice, tannins, blackcurrants. True, it's very dry but it's classy and terrific value.

Chateau la Mauberte Bordeaux 1997
14 C

Possibly the softest and most approachable claret (dry!) you could wish for. Selected stores.

Chateau la Vieille Cure, Fronsac 1995

Better than ever this vintage. Wonderful classic cigar-rich finish. Selected stores.

Chateau les Alberts, Lussac St Emilion 1997
15 D

Nice plump fruit, with some polish to the dry, cracked leather interior.

Chateau Tassin Bordeaux Rouge 1996

Chateau Verdignan Haut-Medoc 1996

A most accomplished, polished claret of some style. Not yet completely as ready to drink as it will be in four or five years, it has great tannin and no mean degree of blackcurrant fruit. Sixty stores.

Chorey Les Beaune, Paul Dugenais 1997　　`13.5` `D`

Claret Cuvee Prestige, Sainsbury's　　`13` `C`

Claret, Sainsbury's　　`12.5` `C`

**Classic Selection Brouilly 1997,
Sainsbury's**　　`14` `D`

**Classic Selection Chateauneuf-du-Pape
1995, Sainsbury's**　　`13.5` `E`

Selected stores.

Clos Magne Figeac, St Emilion 1994　　`16` `E`

Gorgeous rich texture, high class fruit – rich and dry – and
a broad, multifaceted finish. Good now, very good, but will
develop for five to seven years. Selected stores.

Cornas Les Serres Delas Freres 1992　　`14` `G`

Cotes du Rhone NV, Sainsbury's　　`14.5` `B`

Fantastic value: rich, soft, bright and bonny. Selected stores.

**Cotes du Rhone Villages Domaine Michel
Bernard 1997**　　`14` `C`

Very soft and approachable. Selected stores.

**Crozes Hermitage, Cave de Tain
l'Hermitage 1996**　　`14` `D`

**Cuvee Prestige Cotes du Rhone 1996,
Sainsbury's**　　`15` `C`

Gevrey Chambertin Vieilles Vignes 1992

Grenache/Merlot VdP de l'Ardeche, Sainsbury's

Hautes Cotes de Nuits Les Dames Huguettes, Domaine Bertagna 1997

Excellent texture here and huge seriousness of purpose. Classier than many examples at three times the price. Selected stores.

Kressman Monopole Bordeaux Rouge 1996

Dead boring claret. Suit an old field-marshal on his death bed facing his maker (having, in his lifetime, sent a quarter of a million men to their deaths). Such a warrior will find some hellish charm here. So do I – in part. Selected stores.

La Baume Cabernet Sauvignon, VdP d'Oc 1997

Cherries, earth, ripeness, balance, a subtle herbiness and wonderful deep savoury beefy tannins. What a broth! Selected stores.

Les Hauts de Pontet, Pauillac 1995

Merlot VdP d'Oc NV, Sainsbury's (1.5 litre)

Price bracket has been adjusted to the 75cl equivalent.

Merlot VdP de la Cite de Carcassonne, Caroline de Beaulieu 1998

Fantastic leathery tannins, rich ripe fruit (cherries/plums/blackberries), and wonderful dry-edged finish. Hugely elegant and compelling. Selected stores.

Minervois, Sainsbury's `15` `B`

**Philippe de Rothschild Cabernet
Sauvignon d'Oc 1997** `12` `C`

**Philippe de Rothschild Merlot VdP
d'Oc 1997** `13` `C`

**Pinot Noir Joseph de Bel-Air, VdP
d'Oc 1996** `12` `D`

Prieure de Cenac, Cahors 1995 `13.5` `D`

Appley and cindery. Not a six quid wine. The fruit is too austere.
But for Cahors lovers this is a 16-point wine.

Red Burgundy NV, Sainsbury's `12` `D`

**Reserve du Chateau la Garde, Pessac
Leognan 1992** `14.5` `E`

Reserve St Marc Shiraz VdP d'Oc 1997 `15` `C`

**St Joseph Le Grand Pompee, Jaboulet
Ainee 1994** `13.5` `E`

Stowells Claret NV (3-litre box) `10` `C`

Price bracket has been adjusted to the 75cl equivalent.

Syrah VdP d'Oc NV, Sainsbury's `13.5` `B`

**Valreas Domaine de la Grande Bellane
1997** `16` `D`

Ragged yet dainty on its feet, this richly finishing, very dry wine combines a fair spread of hedgerow fruit and delicious tannin. It is classic Rhone Villages red. Great drunk out of a Viking horn or sipped with lievre a la royale.

Vin de Pays de l'Aude Rouge, Sainsbury's 16 B

Tremendous richness and savoury depth here. Hint of leather, hedgerow fruit, tannin. Fantastic. Selected stores.

Vin de Pays des Bouches du Rhone NV, Sainsbury's 14.5 B

Good controlled earthiness, tannins, and a rich, warm finish.

Vin Rouge de France Dry Red Wine, Sainsbury's (3-litre box) 12 B

Price bracket has been adjusted to the 75cl equivalent.

Volnay Chateau Genot-Boulanger 1995 14 G

Vougeot Domaine Bertagna 1995 13 G

FRENCH WINE WHITE

Alsace Blanc de Blancs 1997 14 C

Alsace Gewurztraminer 1997, Sainsbury's 16 D

Even better than the '96! And that was superb. This shows how a rich vintage bestows crispness and spiciness brilliantly in one. 260 stores.

Blanc Anjou, Medium Dry, Sainsbury's

`12` `B`

Blason de Maucaillou Sauvignon, Bordeaux 1997

`16` `C`

Terrific melon and lemon, rich and ripe. Great with all sorts of fish. Unusually good value Bordeaux blanc.

Bordeaux Blanc, Sainsbury's

`14.5` `B`

Utterly simple but delightfully charming. Terrific fresh, clean, gently fruity value.

Bourgogne Chardonnay, Boisset 1997

`13.5` `D`

Chablis Premier Cru 'Les Fourchaumes' 1996

`13.5` `G`

Classic Chablis to begin, then becomes lemonic and new worldish. Too expensive for the style. Eighty stores.

Chardonnay VdP d'Oc, Sainsbury's (3-litre box)

`15` `C`

Price bracket has been adjusted to the 75cl equivalent.

Chateau Carsin, Cadillac 1996 (half bottle)

`15` `D`

Chateau de Cerons 1990 (half bottle)

`13` `E`

Chateau de Chamirey Blanc, Mercurey 1996

`15` `E`

Well, it's just a tenner but it's worth it for the rich chardonnay fruit with that hint of Burgundian vegetality and horny-handed-son-of-the-soil edge. Eighty stores.

Classic Selection Chablis Domaine Sainte Celine 1997, Sainsbury's   13 E

Classic Selection Muscadet de Sevre et Maine Sur Lie 1997, Sainsbury's   13.5 C

May have changed to the '98 vintage by the time this book comes out (yawn).

Classic Selection Pouilly Fuisse 1997, Sainsbury's   13.5 D

Classic Selection Sancerre 1997, Sainsbury's   13.5 D

May have changed to the '98 vintage by the time this book comes out (yawn, yawn).

Clos du Portail, Graves Superieures 1996 (half bottle)   13.5 C

Domaine Belle-Croix, Coteaux de St Bris 1996   13.5 D

Sharp and clean, but picky – good with shellfish. Eighty-four stores.

La Baume Chardonnay VdP d'Oc 1997   16 C

Creamy, subtle, ripe, rich, balanced, delicious – a terrific alternative to sullen white Burgundy. Lovely vegetal, lingering finish – very classy. But may have changed to the '98 vintage by the time this book comes out. 233 stores.

La Baume Sauvignon Blanc, VdP d'Oc 1998   16 C

Can the d'Oc challenge the Kiwis? At this price, yes – though expect less grassiness with the French wine, but the style shines through.

LPA Cotes de St Mont Blanc 1997

Moulin des Groyes, Cotes de Duras Blanc 1997

Muscadet de Sevre et Maine sur Lie NV, Sainsbury's (3-litre box)

Price bracket has been adjusted to the 75cl equivalent.

Muscadet Sevre et Maine Sur Lie, La Goelette 1997 `15` `C`

May have changed to the '98 vintage by the time this book comes out (will it be as chic as the '97).

Orchid Vale Medium French Chardonnay, VdP d'Oc 1997 `13` `C`

Somewhat too obvious for me but for those on the way up from sweet Germans it's a step . . . Selected stores.

Pernand-Vergelesses Domaine Laleure Piot 1996 `13.5` `F`

Pouilly Fume, Cuvee Pierre Louis 1996 `13.5` `E`

Expensive, if typically crisp-edged. Selected stores.

Reserve St Marc Sauvignon Blanc, VdP d'Oc 1997 `16` `C`

An impressively rich sauvignon of class, crispness, softness and great style. May have changed to the '98 vintage by the time this book comes out, but I'll bet it's still crisp.

FRENCH WHITE

Sancerre Domaine la Croix Canat 1997 15 E

One of the neatest Sancerres on sale – real flavour and gooseberry concentration with mineral acids. Selected stores.

Touraine Sauvignon Blanc, Chapelle de Cray 1997 14 C

Vin Blanc de France Dry White Wine, Sainsbury's (3-litre box) 13 B

Price bracket has been adjusted to the 75cl equivalent.

Vin de Pays de l'Aude Blanc, Sainsbury's 15 B

Chipper with healthy fruit. Remarkably clean and fresh, delight-fully impishly fruity wine. 265 stores.

Vin de Pays des Cotes de Gascogne NV, Sainsbury's 15 B

Vouvray la Couronne des Plantagenets 1997 13.5 C

White Burgundy NV, Sainsbury's 14 D

Not bad, for a bourgogne blanc. Has some classic hints. Touch expensive.

GERMAN WINE   WHITE

Bereich Bernkastel Riesling 1997 12 B

Makes an adequate spritzer.

Black Soil Rivaner Riesling 1997 `15` `C`

Blue Nun Liebfraumilch `13` `C`

Dalsheimer Berg Rodenstein Kabinett, Rheinhessen 1997, Sainsbury's `14` `B`

Don't think of it as German. Think of it chilled in summer sitting in a deckchair. It has real charm, this wine.

Fire Mountain Riesling 1997 `14` `C`

Graacher Himmelreich Riesling Spatlese von Kesselstatt 1997 `15` `E`

Keep it for five or six years yet and watch it blossom into a 17.5 point masterpiece of dry-sided honeyed fruit and rich mineralised acids. Sixty-two stores.

Hock NV, Sainsbury's `11.5` `B`

Liebfraumilch NV, Sainsbury's `11` `B`

Mosel, Sainsbury's `14` `B`

Niersteiner Gutes Domtal, Sainsbury's `12` `B`

Oppenheimer Krotenbrunnen Kabinett, Sainsbury's `12.5` `B`

Piesporter Michelsberg, Sainsbury's `12` `B`

Sancta Clara Morio-Muskat, Pfalz 1997 `13.5` `B`

Makes an amusing warm-weather aperitif. Selected stores.

GREEK WINE — RED

Kourtakis Vin de Crete Red 1997 [13] B

GREEK WINE — WHITE

Retsina, Sainsbury's [14] B

HUNGARIAN WINE — WHITE

Family Reserve Gewurztraminer, Mor Region 1997 [13] C

Family Reserve Sauvignon Blanc, Sopron Region 1997 [15] C

ITALIAN WINE — RED

Allora Primitivo, Puglia 1997 [16]

Wonderful strident complexity as the wine flexes its fruity muscles as it flows over the taste buds – it shows many sides of itself including herbs, hedgerows and gripping tannins.

Bardolino Classico 1997, Sainsbury's 13.5 C

Needs to be chilled and drunk with fish.

Chianti Classico, Briante 1996 15 D

Gorgeous richness and ripeness – with all that baked fruit edge of the genre.

Classic Selection Chianti Classico 1996, Sainsbury's 15.5 D

Cherries, baked terracotta earth, ripeness and a rousing finish. Selected stores.

D'Istinto Sangiovese Merlot 1997 (Sicily) 15.5 C

Due Monti Nero di Troia Cabernet Sauvignon Puglia 1996 15.5 C

Fabiano Pinot Noir 1997 11 C

L'Arco Cabernet Franc, Friuli 1997 16.5 C

Fabulous cabernet franc fruit of classically exquisite wild raspberry and slate tannins. Selected stores.

Lambrusco Rosso, Sainsbury's 10 B

Merlot delle Venezie 1997, Sainsbury's 14 C

Montepulciano d'Abruzzo 1997, Sainsbury's 16 C

Terrific, dry, earthy fruit combining herbs, baked earth and ripe plums.

Ripassa, Valpolicella Classico, Zenato 1995 | 15.5 | E

Not as deliciously embittered as the '94 but still lovely stuff with its spicy black cherry fruit and figgy finish.

Rosso di Puglia, Sainsbury's | 14 | B

Sangiovese dell'Umbria, Tenuta di Corbara 1997 | 16.5 | C

Wonderful vigour here from the rich plums and fresh blackcurrants of the fruit to tannins on the finish. A fabulous sangiovese. 180 stores.

Sangiovese di Toscana, Cecchi 1997 | 15 | C

Selvapiana Vigneto Bucerchiale, Chianti Rufina Riserva 1993 | 15.5 | E

Sicilian Red, Sainsbury's | 14 | B

Stowells Montepulciano del Molise NV (3-litre box) | 12 | C

Price bracket has been adjusted to the 75cl equivalent.

Teuzzo Chianti Classico, Cecchi 1995 | 15 | D

Valpolicella Classico 1997, Sainsbury's | 14 | C

Deliciously fruity and cherry-ripe, yet dry to finish.

Valpolicella Classico, Allegrini 1996 | 13 | D

Valpolicella NV, Sainsbury's | 13.5 | B

ITALIAN WINE   WHITE

Allora Chardonnay 1997   `13.5` `C`

Anselmi Soave 1997   `15` `D`

Bianco di Custoza, Geoff Merrill 1997   `14` `C`

Perfectly charming, crisp fish wine. Or with spaghetti a la vongole. May have changed to the '98 vintage by the time this book appears.

**Bianco di Provincia di Verona NV,
Sainsbury's**   `14` `B`

Delicious, soft and gently fruity, hint of raspberry and lime but finishes crisply.

Cecchi Tuscan White NV   `13.5` `C`

Unusual hint of almond to the fruit. 280 stores.

Chardonnay del Salento 1997   `15.5` `D`

Chardonnay i Fossilli 1997   `14.5` `B`

**Classic Selection Frascati Superiore 1997,
Sainsbury's**   `13` `D`

Bit expensive! Selected stores.

Cortese del Piemonte 1997   `15` `C`

**D'Istinto Catarratto Chardonnay 1997
(Sicily)**   `14` `C`

217

Frascati Secco Superiore 1997, Sainsbury's | 13.5 | C

**Garganega IGT delle Venezie 1997,
Sainsbury's** | 13.5 | B

Lambrusco dell'Emilia Bianco. Sainsbury's | 12 | C

Lambrusco Rosato, Sainsbury's | 13 | B

Lambrusco Secco, Sainsbury's | 11 | B

Pinot Grigio Atesino, Sainsbury's | 13 | C

Pinot Grigio Collio 1996 | 15.5 | D

**Rosso di Provincia di Verona NV,
Sainsbury's** | 15 | B

Try it chilled with fish. It's the perfect summer barbecue wine – for meat, veg and fish. Dry earthy cherries, light and lissom.

Sicilian White, Sainsbury's | 13.5 | B

Perfect party wine. Strong enough to withstand acid conversation.

Soave, Sainsbury's | 15.5 | B

**Tenuta di Corbara Orvieto Classico
Superiore 1997** | 15.5 | C

Has that delicious warmth of fruit melded with atypically Italianate nuttiness and crispness. 115 stores.

**Trebbiano di Romagna NV, Sainsbury's
(1.5 litre)** | 13.5 | D

Gently pear-ripe and crisp, with a screw cap. Price bracket has been adjusted to the 75cl equivalent.

LEBANESE WINE   RED

Chateau Musar 1989   12   E

MACEDONIAN WINE   RED

Macedonian Cabernet Sauvignon 1996   13   B

Macedonian Country Red 1996   13.5   B

MACEDONIAN WINE   WHITE

Macedonian Chardonnay 1997   8   B

NEW ZEALAND WINE   WHITE

Montana Sauvignon Blanc 1998   15.5   D

Hints of fatness but finishes cleanly and crisply. Has class and isn't as rich as many Marlborough sauvignons are: it has some finesse.

Shingle Peak Chardonnay, Marlborough 1998 `16.5` `D`

Superb richness and depth of gentle smoky melon fruit. Really stylish and fine. Fifty-two stores.

Shingle Peak Pinot Gris, Marlborough 1998 `16.5` `D`

Superb apricot/peach/orange edged fruit – very fine, very pinot gris – a minor classic of a wine. Ninety-five stores.

Shingle Peak Sauvignon Blanc, Marlborough 1998 `16` `D`

Gorgeous concentration of fruit here, with a lovely zippy finish. 123 stores.

Villa Maria Private Bin Sauvignon, Marlborough 1998 `17` `D`

Back to the form of a few years back when it was the least grassy style of NZ sauvignon yet the most elegant.

PORTUGUESE WINE WHITE

Do Campo Branco, Sainsbury's `14` `B`

Portuguese Rosé, Sainsbury's `13.5` `B`

Vinho Verde, Sainsbury's `13.5` `B`

ROMANIAN WINE · RED

Idle Rock Merlot Reserve 1997 `14` `C`

Idle Rock Pinot Noir Reserve 1997 `13` `C`

River Route Limited Edition Merlot 1997 `15` `C`

Rather claret-like in its dryness but it has a hint of Romanian sun and a hint of spice. Great food wine.

ROMANIAN WINE · WHITE

River Route Chardonnay Limited Edition 1997 `15` `C`

A thick, sticky, very beetle-browed chardonnay, with an acquired jammy richness. It must have rich food to be palatable – like tarragon chicken, prawn risotto, moules with lemon grass and chillies. Selected stores.

SOUTH AFRICAN WINE · RED

Bellingham Merlot 1997 `14` `D`

A sweet merlot. Very slurpable. Not complex. Touch expensive for the style. Selected stores.

Bellingham Shiraz 1997

Fairview Pinotage 1998

Pinotage as elegant, dandyish, refined velvet (yet dry) and sheer deliciousness. 200 stores.

Kumala Cabernet Sauvignon Shiraz 1998

Delicious as both a throat charmer and food companion. It has layers of textured fruit, warm, touch spicy, hint of pepper, good tannins. Lush, luxurious, lissom, lovely to down!

Reserve Selection Merlot 1996, Sainsbury's

South African Pinotage, Sainsbury's

South African Red, Sainsbury's

South African Reserve Selection Cabernet Sauvignon 1996, Sainsbury's

Cosy and warm. Not one hint of cabernet dryness or spiciness except as a departing echo in the throat. Selected stores.

South African Reserve Selection Cabernet Sauvignon/Merlot 1996, Sainsbury's

---

South African Reserve Selection Merlot 1996, Sainsbury's

Superb leathery, smoky ripe fruit with soothing tannins. Terrific stuff for the money. Selected stores.

South African Reserve Selection Pinotage 1998, Sainsbury's

16.5 | D

A high class pinotage which manages to put a brave face on burnt rubber, cassis, pepper, blackberries and dry earthy tannins. 155 stores.

SOUTH AFRICAN WINE   WHITE

Cape Dry White Wine, Sainsbury's

13.5 | B

De Wetshof Estate Lesca Chardonnay 1998

15 | D

One of the Cape's most committed chardonnays. Danie de Wet never makes a bad one, or one wholly unreconciled with charm, and though, like this example, the result is often low key it always provokes the palate.

Mont Rochelle de Villiers Oak Matured Chardonnay 1997

16 | D

Lots of wood but not would-be. It is itself, not a copy (of white burgundy) and has lovely warmth and well-tailored fruit. Sixty-five stores.

South African Chenin Blanc NV, Sainsbury's (3-litre box)

14.5 | B

Price bracket has been adjusted to the 75cl equivalent.

South African Colombard NV, Sainsbury's

14 | C

Good firm fruit. Needs food, I feel.

223

South African Medium Wine, Sainsbury's   11   B

South African Reserve Selection Chardonnay 1998, Sainsbury's   14.5   D

Rounded, rich, ripe and ready – but has underlying elegance. Selected stores.

South African Reserve Selection Sauvignon Blanc 1998, Sainsbury's   16   D

Sauvignon as eager, filthy rich and full of flavour. Selected stores.

South African Sauvignon Blanc, Sainsbury's   15   B

Springfield Estate Special Cuvee Sauvignon Blanc 1998   16   D

A very classy Sancerre in style, but not price. It's superb.

Vergelegen Chardonnay Reserve 1997   16.5   E

Has that great luxury of flavour of the armpit of a massive lottery winner. Sixty stores.

Vergelegen Sauvignon Blanc 1998   15.5   D

Elegance and understatement. Selected stores.

SPANISH WINE   RED

Alicante Tinto, Sainsbury's   15   B

Dama de Toro, Bodegas Farina 1995   `16` `C`

Better than ever in its new vintage. The earthiness is more
refined, the tannins more emollient, the fruit tauter. Selected
stores.

El Conde Oak Aged Vinho de Mesa,
Sainsbury's   `16` `B`

A gorgeously flavoured, cherry-and-vanilla-undertoned wine of
soupy warmth.

Jumilla NV, Sainsbury's   `15.5` `C`

Very soft and sticky but so unabashedly luxurious and flavoursome. Great with food.

La Mancha Castillo de Alhambra 1997,
Sainsbury's   `15` `B`

Bargain fruity tippling here: soft, sweet, deep yet dry. Selected
stores.

Laztana Tempranillo Rioja 1997   `15.5` `B`

Marques de Grinon Valdepusa Syrah 1996   `16.5` `E`

One of the classiest under-a-tenner reds in Spain. It's dry,
spicy, savoury, balanced, rich and very deep. Hugely lingering
flavours.

Navarra, Sainsbury's   `15` `B`

Navarra Tempranillo/Cabernet Sauvignon
Crianza 1995, Sainsbury's   `16` `C`

Wonderful mature fruit here: tobaccoey, ripe, rich, deep, woody,
balanced and very eager to please. Loads of class.

Old Vines Garnacha, Navarra NV 15.5 C

Rioja Reserva Vina Ardanza 1989 14 F

**Stowells Tempranillo La Mancha NV
(3-litre box)** 12.5 B

Price bracket has been adjusted to the 75cl equivalent.

Valencia Oak Aged NV, Sainsbury's 13.5 C

Very plump, ripe and softly rich. Bit emulsion-like but very engaging.

Vinas del Vero Tempranillo/Moristel 1997 14.5 C

SPANISH WINE WHITE

Navarra Rosado NV, Sainsbury's 15 C

USA WINE RED

Black Ridge Carignane/Grenache 1997 14 C

**Bonterra Cabernet Sauvignon 1995
(organic)** 17 E

Sweetly ravishing fruit of such richness and tannic brilliance! Selected stores.

California Estates Old Vine Zinfandel 1996

Individual, rich, vibrant, sexy, deliciously full, deep and softly structured, this wine is a wonderful zinfandel with loads of juicy raspberry, plum and black cherry flavour. The perfume and the finish are lingering and very complex. Ravishing stuff, gooey but huge fun. Not at all stores.

Coastal Pinot Noir, Robert Mondavi 1996

Smells of well-hung grouse and there's even a hint of truffle in there. The fruit is awesomely compacted and ripe compared with any Burgundy of the same price and the performance of the fruit as it rolls itself across the tongue is delightful. Classic pinot of personality and huge appeal to the pinot aficionado. A real treat. Selected stores.

Eagle Peak Merlot, Fetzer Vineyards 1997

Decidedly chewy yet very soft and warm. Curious paradox of styles: seems composty and ripe then goes dry and tannin-teasing, blackcurrant beneath its feet. Delicious stuff. 139 stores.

Oakville Robert Mondavi Cabernet Sauvignon 1993

Lot of money but then it's a lot of wine. It's more energetic yet intellectually charged than many a first growth claret, fifteen years older, at four times the price. The sheer finesse of the leather, tobacco, wood, vegetality, cassis and lush rich tannins make it a supremely entertaining mouthful. A complete wine of wide charm and ineffable Californian vivacity. Eighteen stores only.

Sutter Home Merlot 1997

Touch sweet on the finish. Selected stores.

USA WINE WHITE

Byron Chardonnay, Santa Barbara County 1996

Enormously pricey but full of personality and rich, ripe yet balanced fruit. It has undoubted class and smugly knows it, but Fetzer at half the price is no less regal. Fifty-seven stores.

Fetzer Bonterra Chardonnay 1996 (organic)

Rivetingly rich, rampant, creamy, woody, balanced and flamboyant – but so elegant with it! It's like a Vivienne Westwood man's shirt – subtly outrageous. Selected stores.

Fetzer Sundial Chardonnay 1997

Always as full of sun as the face of a California beach bum, this is fruit modelled on richness, warmth, and the flavours of the tropics. Eighty stores.

Gallo Colombard NV

Garnet Point Chardonnay Chenin Blanc 1997

Very warm and fruity, hint of muskiness to the ripe melon. As easy to drink as breathing.

FORTIFIED WINE

Aged Amontillado, Sainsbury's (half bottle)   `13.5`   `B`

Blandy's Duke of Clarence Madeira   `15.5`   `E`

Gonzales Byass Matusalem Old Oloroso (half bottle)   `14`   `E`

Medium Dry Montilla, Sainsbury's   `13.5`   `B`

Mick Morris Rutherglen Liqueur Muscat (half bottle)   `17`   `C`

A miraculously richly textured pud wine of axle-grease texture and creamy figginess. Huge, world class. Sixty selected stores only.

Old Oloroso, Sainsbury's (half bottle)   `16`   `B`

Pale Cream Montilla, Sainsbury's   `14`   `B`

Pale Cream Sherry, Sainsbury's   `15.5`   `C`

Pale Dry Amontillado, Sainsbury's   `15`   `C`

Pale Dry Fino Sherry, Sainsbury's   `15`   `D`

Pale Dry Manzanilla, Sainsbury's   `15`   `C`

Pale Dry Montilla, Sainsbury's   14   B

Palo Cortado, Sainsbury's (half bottle)   16   B

Be different. A winter warmer of quirkily nutty richness yet not sweetness. Not at all stores.

Ruby Port, Sainsbury's   13   D

Sainsbury's LBV Port 1992   15.5   E

Wonderful sweet fruit here. Superb value for money.

Tawny Port, Sainsbury's   13.5   D

Ten Year Old Tawny Port, Sainsbury's   15   E

A brilliant start to a winter's evening. So wait for winter.

SPARKLING WINE/CHAMPAGNE

Asti, Sainsbury's (Italy)   13   C

Australian Chardonnay/Pinot Noir Brut 1992, Sainsbury's   14   D

Some lean elegance here. Ninety stores.

Blanc de Noirs Champagne NV, Sainsbury's   16   F

One of the best value champagnes around. Really elegant.

Cava Rosado, Sainsbury's · 14 · C

Has a cherry-edge to the crisp fruit.

Cava, Sainsbury's · 16.5 · C

Still a flagship sparkling wine: crisp, clean, fresh, classic. Better than hundreds of champagnes.

Champagne Chanoine 1990 · 16 · G

Compelling stuff – a special parcel for the Millennium. 125 stores.

Champagne Demi-Sec NV, Sainsbury's · 14 · F

Lot of fruit for a bubbly but it works! Try it well chilled as a summer aperitif. It's better than many a rosé. Selected stores.

Champagne Pol Roger Brut 1990 · 13 · H

170 stores.

Champagne Premier Cru Extra Dry, Sainsbury's (1.5 litre) · 15 · G

Brilliant bulk. Great sexy bottle. The price bracket has been adjusted to reflect the bottle equivalent. 135 stores.

Chardonnay Brut, Methode Traditionelle, Sainsbury's (France) · 14 · D

Freixenet Cava Rosado NV · 14 · D

Gallo Brut · 10 · D

Graham Beck Brut NV (South Africa) · 14 · D

Crisp and gently fruity.

Grand Cru Millennium Champagne Brut, Sainsbury's `15` `G`

Delicious classy fruit. Selected stores.

Jacobs Creek Chardonnay/Pinot Noir Brut NV (Australia) `13` `D`

Light and fruity. Selected stores.

Lindauer Special Reserve NV (New Zealand) `14` `E`

Millennium Vintage Cava 1997, Sainsbury's `11` `D`

Rather disappointing for such precious presentation.

Seaview Brut NV (Australia) `14` `D`

Lithe and light. Delicious simplicity.

Seaview Brut Rosé NV (Australia) `14` `D`

Delicate little rosé.

Segura Viudas Brut Reserva (Spanish) `13` `D`

Sekt, Medium Dry, Sainsbury's (Germany) `13` `C`

Sparkling White Burgundy, Sainsbury's `13.5` `D`

Vin Mousseux Brut, Sainsbury's (France) `13` `C`

J Sainsbury plc
Stamford House
Stamford Street
London SE1 9LL
Tel 0171 921 6000
Fax 0171 921 7925

SOMERFIELD

ARGENTINIAN WINE   RED

Argentine Country Red NV, Somerfield | 14.5 | B

Soupy yet far from simply all-fruit-not-for-the-squeamish. It has a dry, rich edge of some charm. More gauche than gaucho, perhaps, but entertaining.

Bright Brothers Argentine Tempranillo 1997 | 15 | C

Bright Brothers San Juan Cabernet Sauvignon 1998 | 17.5 | C

Utterly magically alive and alert wine which opens up such rich savoury depths as it lingers on the taste buds. It's exotic yet classic, beautifully textured and compellingly well finished off. A fantastic fiver's worth.

Santa Julia Sangiovese 1998 | 14.5 | C

Delicious cheekily plummy wine of massive lapupability.

Santa Julia Tempranillo 1998 | 16.5 | C

What utter chutzpah! It's simply wonderful! It makes a billion riojas seem like antique crones.

ARGENTINIAN WINE   WHITE

Argentine White NV, Somerfield | 14.5 | B

Terrific value quaffing: has style, flavour, modernity and crispness.

**Bright Brothers San Juan Chardonnay
Reserve 1998**

AUSTRALIAN WINE

**Australian Cabernet Shiraz 1998,
Somerfield**

Rollingly rich and frolicsome.

Australian Dry Red, Somerfield

Delicious! Delicious! Delicious! Did you get that? I said . . . oh,
never mind.

Basedow Barossa Shiraz 1996 16 E

Minty cherries and plum, soft tannin, rich deep finish. A hugely
drinkable wine of substance and style.

**Hardys Nottage Hill Cabernet Sauvignon/
Shiraz 1998** 16 D

Loads of savoury plums and blackberries with lovely earthy
tannins. Scrumptious drinking here.

Hardys Stamp Shiraz Cabernet 1998

Lovely rich and bright and a touch emulsion-like in texture.
But it has balance and savoury ripeness. It's a great food wine.

Penfolds Coonawarra Bin 128 Shiraz 1994

Getting a bit ragged now that the tannins have overtaken the
sugars. Very dry and sulky.

Penfolds Koonunga Hill Shiraz Cabernet Sauvignon 1997   14 D

Rosemount Estate Shiraz 1997   16.5 E

Massively mouth-filling and rampant. Almost an alien construct compared to similar graped Rhone reds. Top 150 stores.

Rosemount Estate Shiraz Cabernet 1998   15.5 D

So deliciously sweet and fruity: soft and full yet delicate on the finish. Deliciously approachable and warm.

AUSTRALIAN WINE   WHITE

Australian Chardonnay 1998, Somerfield   16.5 C

Rich, smoky, developed, full and rich – hints of nut. Ripe but not too rampant. A lovely wine of great flavour.

Australian Dry White 1998, Somerfield   16 B

Superb value for money here, indeed astonishing: rich, fresh, classy, plump yet lissom, this is lovely wine of style and decisiveness.

Australian Semillon/Chardonnay 1998, Somerfield   14 C

Very sticky and ripe – needs Thai food or roasted chillied chicken wings.

Banrock Station Chenin/Chardonnay 1998   12 B

Basedow Barossa Chardonnay 1997

Chardonnay in the rich, buttery, oily, baked yet balanced Aussie style. Utterly wonderful tippling here.

Hardys Chardonnay Sauvignon Blanc 1997

A very assertive companion of gently sticky fruit. Wonderful wine for shellfish dishes with rich sauces. Top 150 stores.

Hardys Padthaway Chardonnay 1996

Do you like Meursault? You'll like this, then. This kind of woody, hay-rich, vegetal fruitiness is a miracle under eight quid. Top 200 stores.

Hardys Stamp Semillon/Chardonnay 1998

Superb medley of fruits in firm adult display. Loads of richness and runaway depth but not remotely over-the-top.

Jacobs Creek Semillon/Chardonnay 1998

Old warhorse still good value and richly fruity (but balanced).

Lindemans Bin 65 Chardonnay 1998

Supremely sure of itself, this well-established brand showing, in its '98 manifestation, what a great year this is for Aussie whites from the region (Hunter Valley). This has great hints of warm fruit balanced by complex crispness and acidity. A lovely under-a-fiver bobby dazzler.

Penfolds Bin 202 Riesling 1998

Will rapidly improve over the next year and should achieve a high level of complexity. Already in swaddling clothes it's deliciously mineral-tinged and elegantly fruity.

Penfolds Koonunga Hill Chardonnay 1998 · 16.5 · D

What a great brand! Stunning richness and balanced, classy finish. If only white burgundians at three times the price could be this good.

Penfolds Rawsons Retreat Semillon/ Chardonnay/Colombard 1998 · 15.5 · C

Has lovely deft balance: the fruit holds the acidity in a gorgeous embrace.

Penfolds The Valleys Chardonnay 1998 · 16.5 · D

Delicate yet potent, rich yet unshowy, balanced yet full-frontal and unashamedly hedonistic. A lovely wine.

St Hilary Padthaway Chardonnay 1997 · 15 · E

Not the most elegant expression of the '97 chardonnay harvest but it has character and a subtly chewy texture. Top 150 stores.

BULGARIAN WINE · RED

Bulgarian Cabernet Sauvignon 1997, Somerfield · 15.5 · B

Brilliant value. Not for the classicist perhaps but it's got lovely plummy fruit and firm tannins.

Domaine Boyar Special Reserve Cabernet Sauvignon, Oriachovitza 1994 · 15.5 · C

Plummy, ripe, dry, balanced – you can spend lots more and get lots less.

Iambol Bulgarian Merlot 1997 · 15.5 · B

Superb value – real hints of merlot's classic leatheriness but in a fresh, new, polished form.

BULGARIAN WINE · WHITE

Barrel Fermented Chardonnay, Pomorie 1997 · 14 · C

Chewy and lemony. Top 150 stores.

Bulgarian Chardonnay 1998, Somerfield · 15.5 · B

Utterly delicious: smoky aroma, superbly lemonic fruit. Terrific!

Domaine Boyar Barrel Fermented Chardonnay 1996 · 14.5 · C

Suhindol Aligote Chardonnay Country White, Somerfield · 14 · B

Bit fresh: but fish will love its bony features.

CHILEAN WINE · RED

Chilean Cabernet Sauvignon 1997, Somerfield · 16.5 · C

Oh what nerve! It offers all of a great Bordeaux's tannins but none of the austere fruit. It's simply terrific.

Chilean Merlot 1998, Somerfield · 16.5 · C

Lovely rich warmth to the texture, ripeness to the fruit and a whiplash clean fruity finish of elegant leather.

Chilean Red 1998, Somerfield · 15.5 · B

Compulsively slurpworthy softness and lovely dry lingering fruit.

La Palmeria Cabernet Sauvignon Merlot Reserve 1998 · 16.5 · D

Gorgeous sweetness yet dryness, class yet consummate drinkability, style yet unpretentiousness – it's a lovely, rich, textured wine of stunning concentration.

Terra Noble Merlot 1997 · 17.5 · C

What a tremendous price for such wonderfully soft leathery fruit (cherries, blackcurrants and plums) and such superb warmth and texture to it. It's a wonderful wine of huge class and depth. It'll manage either food or mood magnificently. Top 100 stores.

CHILEAN WINE · WHITE

Chilean Chardonnay 1998, Somerfield · 16 · C

Woody complexity, hint of vegetality, persistence of rich fruit and clean acids – is this a bargain or what?

Chilean Sauvignon Blanc 1998, Somerfield · 15 · C

A lovely hint of dry, grassy, fresh gooseberry fruit.

Chilean White 1998, Somerfield

Thunderingly tasty bargain on all fronts: fruit, balance with acidity, class and fresh finish.

Cono Sur Viognier 1998

Lovely apricot aroma but the fruit is more in the lemon line. I'd be inclined to cellar this wine for three or four years to develop and become an 18-pointer and possibly in the Condrieu class. Top 150 stores.

FRENCH WINE RED

Beaumes de Venise Carte Noire, Cotes du Rhone Villages 1997

Brilliant earthy fruit. Loads of hedgerow personality and purposeful finishing power.

Bourgogne, Hautes-Cotes de Bourgogne Rouge 1997

Bourilly, Selles 1998

Buzet Cuvee 44 1997

Chateau Blanca, Bordeaux 1997

Chateau Cazal-Viel Cuvee des Fees Vieilles Vignes, St Chinian 1997

Wonderful! Drenched in tobacco and herbs which slowly resonate on the taste buds like a sustained bass chord.

Chateau de Caraghuiles, Corbieres 1996 `14` `C`

One of the best value organic reds around – in this vintage, riper and a touch sweeter.

Chateau Pierredon, Bordeaux Superieur 1995 `14` `D`

Chateau Plaisance, Montagne St Emilion 1996 `15.5` `D`

Chateau Saint Robert, Graves 1996 `15` `D`

Chateau Talence, Premieres Cotes de Bordeaux 1997 `13.5` `D`

Chateau Valoussiere, Coteaux du Languedoc 1996 `16` `C`

Like a minor claret of a great year (plus a herby undertone of savoury richness).

Claret, Somerfield `12` `B`

Corbieres Rouge Val d'Orbieu, Somerfield `15.5` `B`

Terrific! Tasty, taut, tangy, tantalising! (Price suits to a T, too.)

Cotes de Gascogne Rouge 1998, Somerfield `13.5` `B`

Cotes de Roussillon NV, Somerfield `13.5` `B`

Domaine de Bisconte, Cotes du Roussillon 1996

14 C

Very very ripe – super-ripe, and as such it needs food to embrace it.

Domaine la Tuque Bel Air, Cotes de Castillon 1997

14 D

Handsome little claret. Good with barbecued lamb chops.

Fitou Rocher d'Ambree 1998, Somerfield

13.5 C

Gigondas Chateau St Andre 1997

15 D

Big bonny bouncing fruit of lushly controlled meaty depth.

Goutes et Couleurs Syrah Mourvedre 1997

 16 C

Wonderful rich warm fruit – hint of spice and tannin but emphatic elegance and easy tippling.

Gouts et Couleurs Syrah Mourvedre VdP d'Oc 1997

14 C

Hautes Cotes de Beaune, Georges Desire 1996

12 D

James Herrick Cuvee Simone VdP d'Oc 1997

16 C

Such elegant textured richness. It's on a high level of class, this wine.

Laperouse Syrah Cabernet 1996

 16 C

Mature and warmly textured, gently savoury and hedgerow fruity. Good tannins. At the peak of its drinkability.

Medoc, Somerfield | 10 | C

Merlot VdP d'Oc 1998, Somerfield | 14.5 | B

Most accomplished sense of balance between acid/fruit/tannins.
Boring description? Yes, sorry.

Oak Aged Claret, Somerfield | 13 | C

Red Burgundy 1997, Somerfield | 11 | D

Sirius Bordeaux Rouge 1996 | 14 | D

Getting more personality as it ages. Not a bad little claret
now.

Vacqueyras Domaine le Brussiere 1998 | 14 | C

Ripely forward in to the breech.

**Vin de Pays des Bouches du Rhone Red
1998, Somerfield** | 13.5 | B

Sticky, rich and ripe. Bit too much for me. (It's like emulsion.)

Winter Hill VdP de l'Aude Rouge 1998 | 15 | B

Gorgeous dry cherry/plum ripe fruit.

FRENCH WINE   WHITE

**Alsace Blanc de Blancs, Caves de
Turckheim NV** | 14 | C

Lovely summer aperitif and barbecued fish wine. Has class and
hauteur.

Anjou Blanc 1998, Somerfield `12` `B`

Touch sweetish.

Bordeaux Clairet 1998 `13` `C`

Bordeneuve Blanc VdP des Cotes de Gascogne 1998, Somerfield `13` `C`

Bourgogne Haute Cotes de Beaune, Cottin Blanc 1997 `13` `D`

Chablis 1997, Somerfield `12.5` `E`

Chardonnay VdP d'Oc 1998, Somerfield `13.5` `C`

Chardonnay VdP du Jardin de la France 1998 `14` `C`

Very fresh and knife-edge keen to finish. A wine for shellfish.

Domaine du Bois Viognier, VdP d'Oc Maurel Vedeau 1998 `15` `D`

Very rich yet never overdone or blowsy – elegant and cool.

Domaine Ste Agathe Oak Aged Chardonnay, VdP d'Oc Maurel Vedeau 1998 `16` `D`

Oozes class and subtle fruit flavours – a lovely welcoming wine.

Entre Deux Mers 1998, Somerfield `13` `C`

Bit flabby on the finish.

Gewurztraminer Alsace, Caves de Turckheim 1998 `15` `D`

Superb summer wine, with its spicy, crushed rose-petal fruit, but this specimen will also age for two or three years *and* improve greatly.

James Herrick Chardonnay 1997 `16` `C`

One of southern France's most accomplished, classically styled, bargain chardonnays.

Laperouse Chardonnay VdP d'Oc 1996 `15.5` `C`

Lovely woody undertones of a mature chardonnay – bit white Burgundy-like and rather a snip at this price. Top 150 stores.

Les Marionettes Marsanne, VdP d'Oc 1997 `15.5` `C`

Rich and ripe, warm and food-friendly.

Muscat de Frontignan NV (50 cl) `17` `C`

Fantastic accompaniment to pastry desserts: it's creamy, toffeed, caramel-edged, hugely honeyed and husky and it tastes like a drink you could offer to a goddess (before you ask her to live with you).

Rivers Meet Sauvignon/Semillon, Bordeaux 1998 `13` `C`

Very grassy undertone.

Vin de Pays Comte Tolosan 1998, Somerfield `14` `B`

Just plain, crisp, good-value glugging.

249

**Vin de Pays des Coteaux de l'Ardeche
White 1998, Somerfield**   `13.5`   `B`

Vouvray 1998, Somerfield   `13.5`   `C`

Medium sweet aperitif.

White Burgundy 1997, Somerfield   `13`   `C`

GERMAN WINE   WHITE

Baden Dry NV, Somerfield   `13`   `C`

Plain and simple.

Baden Gewurztraminer NV   `14`   `C`

Good Chinese food wine. Great with duck, rice, noodles etc.

Hock, Somerfield   `12`   `B`

Mix with Perrier and ice for a lovely summer spritzer (15.5 points).

Morio Muskat, St Ursula NV   `14`   `B`

Mosel Riesling Halbtrocken NV   `14`   `B`

**Niersteiner Spiegelberg, Riesling Kabinett
Rudolph Muller, Somerfield**   `13.5`   `B`

Needs spritzering to kill the sugar.

Rheingau Riesling 1996 `13` `C`

Rheinhessen Auslese NV, Somerfield `13` `C`

Rudesheimer Rosengarten NV, Somerfield `14` `B`

Brilliant value summer aperitif. Try it well chilled in a deckchair (essential to appreciate this wine to the full).

Schloss Schonborn Riesling Kabinett 1987 `15.5` `D`

St Johanner Abtey Kabinett, Rudolph Muller NV `13` `B`

Falls a bit short but has a nice chewy edge. Spritzer candidate.

St Ursula Dry Riesling 1998 `14` `C`

A brilliant summer aperitif. Taut and dry and chewy.

GREEK WINE WHITE

Samos Greek Muscat NV (half bottle) `15.5` `B`

HUNGARIAN WINE WHITE

Castle Ridge Pinot Grigio, Neszmely 1997 `13` `C`

Top 150 stores.

ITALIAN WINE   RED

Bricco Zanone Barbera d'Asti 1997   14   C

Lovely uncompromised Italiante sweetness and dry richness.

Chianti Classico Montecchio 1996   14   D

Cherries and plums and nice dollops of earth. Good food wine.

D'Istinto Sangiovese/Merlot 1997 (Sicily)   15.5   C

I Grilli di Thalia 1997 (Sicily)   14   C

Juicier than previous vintages.

L'Arco Cabernet Franc, Friuli 1996   15.5   C

Le Trulle Primitivo del Salento 1997   16.5   C

Dark and delicious, rich and ripe, beautifully no-nonsense and well cut, this is a tremendous wine for mood or food.

Mimosa Maremma Sangiovese 1997   16   C

Fantastically earthy-edged, rich, deep, dry, clotted and captivatingly fruity wine of great charm. An outstanding barbecued-meat wine.

Monrubio Sangiovese, Umbria 1997   15   C

Not remotely like the Tuscan example of this grape, this has richness, gripping tannins, and subdued hedgerow fruit. Top 150 stores.

Montepulciano d'Abruzzo Madonna dei Miracoli 1997, Somerfield

15.5 | **C**

Piccini Chianti Classico 1996

11 | **D**

Soltero Rosso, Settesoli 1995 (Sicily)

14 | **C**

Terralle, Primitivo di Puglia 1997, Somerfield

16.5 | **C**

Oh, what wonderfully chewy, savoury, soft, rich, dry, very classy and highly individual fruit. Marvellous mouthful.

Valpolicella Classico, Vigneti Casterna 1996

14 | **C**

Good summer barbecue wine – has hedgerow ripeness plus dry tannins. Top 150 stores.

ITALIAN WINE WHITE

Bianco di Puglia 1998, Somerfield

13.5 | **B**

Bright Brothers Greganico/Chardonnay 1998

15.5 | **C**

Delightfully crisp and clear-headed wine of charm and consummate drinkability.

D'Istinto Insolia Trebbiano 1998 13 B

Le Vele Verdicchio di Castello di Jesi
Classico 1998 13 C

Marche Bianco 1998, Somerfield 14 B

Hints of raspberry to the gentle citricity. A grand little thirst-quencher.

Sicilian White 1998. Somerfield 14 B

Richly flavoured and thickly knitted in texture. A barbecued fish wine.

NEW ZEALAND WINE WHITE

Coopers Creek Chardonnay, Gisborne
1998 16.5 E

Consummate class in a glass here: dry, fruity, calm, elegant, ripe, balanced, precise and total, utter quaffing quality of the highest order. Top 150 stores.

Coopers Creek Sauvignon Blanc,
Marlborough 1998 13.5 E

Shows the fatness of finish of the Marlborough '98s and as such lacks elegance and value. But make no mistake, it is still highly drinkable. Top 150 stores.

Montana Sauvignon Blanc 1998 15.5 D

Hints of fatness but finishes cleanly and crisply. Has class and isn't as rich as many Marlborough sauvignons are: it has some finesse.

Timara Dry White 1998

One of the few Kiwis I am less than over-the-moon about.

PORTUGUESE WINE RED

Alta Mesa Red, Ribatejo 1997

Terrific posture! Sits up straight and true – muscled, lithe, fleshy.

Atlantic Vines Bright Brothers Baga 1997

Very bright (by name and nature). Delicious chilled with a fish stew.

Bright Brothers Trincadeira Preta, Ribatejo 1997

Fiuza Bright Cabernet Sauvignon 1996 `16` `C`

Classic green pepper aroma and hint of black pepper and this edginess is carried through to the rich, rippling fruit. Lovely wine. Top 150 stores.

Portada 1997

Ripe cherries, crisp apple, mature plums – about do for you? (Does for me.)

Portuguese Red 1998, Somerfield   `15` `B`

Great, soft, plummy thing! So cuddly and endearing and stuffed with fruit.

PORTUGUESE WINE   WHITE

Fiuza Bright Chardonnay, Ribatejo 1998   `15.5` `C`

Starts full and rich, then gets mellow and discreet, but it has finesse, class and persistence and is a bargain bottle. Top 150 stores.

Portuguese White 1998, Somerfield   `15` `B`

A proud fish and chips wine.

ROMANIAN WINE   RED

Pietrossa Young Vatted Cabernet
Sauvignon 1997   `15` `C`

Romanian Rovit Pinot Noir 1995   `15` `B`

Well, it isn't pinot as snobs (or you and I) know it, but it's a thoroughly heartening glug of distinct drinkability.

Romanian Special Reserve Merlot,
Sahateni 1992   `16.5` `C`

Snap it up! This is serious, dry, very dry merlot of tension, tannins, tenacity and texture. Wonderful good food glugging. Top 150 stores.

SOUTH AFRICAN WINE — RED

Bellingham Pinotage 1997 | 15 | D |

Sweet and lush, hint of wild strawberry. Top 150 stores.

Bush Vines Pinotage 1998, Somerfield | 16 | C |

Gorgeous hints of cherry pie, plums, licorice and nuts – like an unusually forward Amarone. Wonderful wine. Fantastic price.

Cape Red 1998, Somerfield | 16 | H |

What a wonderful house red! It may bring the house down but you will be protected. This wine is an elixir – it wards off evil.

Kumala Cinsault Pinotage 1998 | 15 | C |

Chewy, ripe, wonderfully fruity and hedgerow sweet.

Kumala Reserve Cabernet Sauvignon 1997 | 17 | E |

Wonderful one-off marvel of sublime cabernet class: pepper, cheroots, blackberries, tannins – it's got the lot. Plus superb textured richness. Top 150 stores.

South African Cabernet Sauvignon NV, Somerfield | 16 | C |

Classic peppery edge to some ripe and very deep wine of great charm and concentration. It has a sense of being an old-fashioned claret but cloaking this respectability is some real, rampant, new world richness.

South African Cinsault Cabernet 1998, Somerfield

Very juicy and soft – drinkable. Good chilled with fish.

South African Pinotage 1998, Somerfield

Baked rubber, cheroots, plum – a classic dry pinotage!!! Drink it all before Christmas! It's too wonderfully youthful to appreciate middle age – except with the throat it will pour down. A terrific pinotage of depth and deftness.

SOUTH AFRICAN WINE WHITE

Bellingham Sauvignon Blanc 1998

Fresh and frisky to finish – good rich fruit opens up this attractive display. Top 150 stores.

Bush Vines Colombard 1998

Bit brutal and fresh at first tasting. It needs six months in this country to mellow, when I suspect a 15-point wine will emerge.

South African Chardonnay 1998, Somerfield

Improving slightly in bottle.

South African Colombard 1998, Somerfield

Lovely melon/lemon double act.

South African Dry White 1998, Somerfield

SPANISH WINE RED

Berberana Rioja Tempranillo 1997

Classic vanilla edge (American wood) but it's not too dry or sulky but silken and fresh.

Bright Brothers Navarra Garnacha 1997

Terrific throughput of fruit here: style, depth, richness and a measure of cool class.

Pergola Tempranillo, Manchuela 1998, Somerfield

A delightfully unpretentiously rich and full wine (blackcurrants and dry cherries) but it has serious dry intentions on the finish.

Rioja Tinto Almaraz NV, Somerfield

Terrific value Rioja! Handsome fruit here.

Sierra Alta Cabernet Sauvignon 1998

High indeed! Proof that Spain can take on Chile. A wonderful wine of great class and style, huge depth and richness, and superb tannins. It's fresh, seriously complex and delightfully unfussy!

Sierra Alta Tempranillo 1997

Valencia Red, Somerfield

Stunningly rich value for money. Baked plum, hint of apple skin, good no-nonsense tannins.

SPANISH WINE WHITE

Castillo Imperial Blanco 1998, Somerfield

Terrific fresh fruit here.

Moscatel de Valencia, Somerfield

Superb, rich fruit here, great with dessert, of cloying texture, candied melon, honeyed fruit. And a screw-cap too! No filthy tree bark!

Muscatel de Valencia, Somerfield

Hint of marmalade, lashings of honey and hint of strawberry jam. What a bargain pud wine this is. And its screw cap ensures it stays fresh and frisky.

Pergola Oak Aged Viura, Manchuela 1997, Somerfield

Great value lemony fruit.

Santa Catalina Verdejo/Sauvignon 1998, Somerfield

Excellent richness and flavour, touch less impactful on the finish but overall it deserves its rating because of its class.

URUGUAYAN WINE — RED

Bright Brothers Cabernet Franc Tannat 1998 `15.5` `C`

Unusually delicious meaty aroma, unusual blend of grapes and altogether a triumph of blending. Terrific stuff – better than a million Beaujolais, which its fresh-faced plumpness resembles.

USA WINE — RED

Californian Dry Red, Somerfield `14` `C`

Gallo Turning Leaf Cabernet Sauvignon 1995 `15` `D`

Laguna Canyon Zinfandel 1997 `15` `C`

USA WINE — WHITE

Californian Colombard/Chardonnay, Somerfield `13.5` `C`

Garnet Point Chenin Chardonnay 1997 `15.5` `C`

Wonderful plump fruit here. As easy to drink as breathing.

Redwood Chardonnay 1996 15 D

Talus Chardonnay 1997 16 D

So warm and rich, yet dry and balanced, that you do wonder at the price. Not, perhaps, as Californian-elegant as some – but the neo-rusticity of this is terrific. Top 200 stores.

FORTIFIED WINE

Fine Old Amontillado Sherry, Somerfield 14.5 C

Fino Luis Caballero, Somerfield 16.5 C

Gorgeous bone-dry fruit: saline, almondy, tea-leafy – it's sheer classic Spanish tippling. Great with grilled prawns fresh from the barbecue.

Manzanilla Gonzales Byass, Somerfield 14.5 C

Superior Cream Sherry, Somerfield 12 C

SPARKLING WINE/CHAMPAGNE

Asti Spumante, Somerfield 12 D

Australian Sparkling NV, Somerfield 16.5 D

Lovely plumpness yet finesse. It's a really scrummy bubbly.

Cremant de Bourgogne, Caves de Bailly 1995   `16` `D`

What a bargain! As dryly, wryly expressive as many a Champagne at four times the price.

Devauzelle Champagne NV   `13.5` `F`

Huguenot Hills Sparkling NV   `14` `D`

This is the same wine as the Somerfield South African Sparkling Sauvignon, (qv) – the new label will be coming into store as this book comes out.

Huguenot Hills Sparkling (South Africa)   `14` `D`

Lindauer Brut NV (New Zealand)   `14.5` `E`

Expressive of nothing but great value for money and utterly charming sipping.

Millennium Champagne 1990, Somerfield   `13` `G`

Don't buy it unless you are certifiably unbalanced in the pocket. Yes, it's drinkable but Somerfield has better bubblies for a lot less dosh.

Moscato Fizz, Somerfield   `14.5` `C`

Mumm Cuvee Napa Brut (California)   `16` `E`

So much more assertive, refined, tasty and sanely priced than its French cousins I'm surprised there aren't serious riots in Rheims.

Nicolas Feuillate Brut Premier Cru NV   `14` `G`

Difficult to rate such insouciance and style any lower. Top 150 stores.

Nottage Hill Sparkling Chardonnay `14.5` `D`

Nottage Hill Sparkling Chardonnay 1997 (Australia) `15.5` `D`

Perfumed and stylish with a lovely undercurrent of fruit.

Pierre Larousse Chardonnay Brut NV (France) `16` `C`

Superb value for money. Has good rich fruit but it's serious and dry and not remotely tart or blowsy. Real bargain elegance here.

Prince William Blanc de Blancs Champagne NV, Somerfield `13` `G`

Top 150 stores.

Prince William Champagne 1er Cru, Somerfield `12.5` `F`

Prince William Champagne Rosé NV, Somerfield `13` `G`

Seaview Brut Rosé `14` `D`

Delicate little rosé.

Seaview Pinot Noir Chardonnay 1994 `15` `E`

Seaview Pinot Noir/Chardonnay 1994 (Australia) `16` `E`

One of Australia's strongest and tastiest challenges to Rheim's hegemony.

Somerfield Cava Brut NV

Elegant, not coarse, taut, wimpish or blowsy, but has hints of ripe fruit and a restrained edge. Fantastic value.

Somerfield Rosé Cava NV

Great fun – and better than many a pink champagne at twice the price. Stunning value here.

South African Sparkling Sauvignon, Somerfield

Gorgeous, just gorgeous! Loads of personality and flavour – yet it's stylish withal.

Somerfield
Gateway House
Hawkfield Business Park
Whitchurch Lane
Bristol BS14 0TJ
Tel 0117 9359359
Fax 0117 9780629

TESCO

ARGENTINIAN WINE RED

Bright Brothers San Juan Reserve Cabernet/Shiraz 1998

Very juicy and ripe but excellent food wine. Top 200 stores.

Bright Brothers San Juan Reserve Shiraz 1998

Bright and breezy, ripe yet dry, hint of minestrone as it finishes. Top 200 stores.

Chimango Tempranillo Malbec NV

Fruity and rich, that's about it. Not at all stores.

Monster Spicy Red Syrah 1998, Tesco

Fabulous! And it's spicy and deep and intense. A lovely rip-roaring, juicy wine with a dry underbelly of insistent richness and classiness. Great stuff.

Norton Malbec 1996

Brilliant vegetality, textured richness and depth of tannicity. Great food wine. This has come on immeasurably in bottle since I first tasted it early in '98. Top 200 stores.

Norton Privada 1996

Odd but convincing. Huge depth of tannins and rich fruit. Strikes wondrously deep – great stuff! Top eighty-five stores.

Picajuan Peak Bonarda NV

Picajuan Peak Malbec NV

Picajuan Peak Sangiovese NV

'Q' Tempranillo 1997

Astonishing level of juicy, creamy, ripe richness here. Hint of vanilla, touch of plum and wild strawberry – utterly yummy. Top eighty stores.

Santa Julia Cabernet Sauvignon Oak Reserve 1996

Wonderful layers of juicy richness and dry tannins beautifully intermingled. Immediacy, class, concentration and sheer velvet deliciousness. Top 200 stores.

Santa Julia Malbec Oak Reserve 1996

Leathery and very tannic. Deep, rich, and hugely nose-filling. You really do feel here that you've bitten off more than you can chew – but you chew it. Top eighty-five stores.

Santa Julia Montepulciano Oak Reserve 1998

So deliciously meaty and ripe, dry and dangerous – it's sheer crumpled velvet and vivacious fruit. Top eighty stores.

ARGENTINIAN WINE WHITE

Picajuan Peak Chardonnay NV

Not as exciting as in previous non-vintage blends.

Picajuan Peak Viognier NV `15.5` `C`

AUSTRALIAN WINE

Australian Cabernet/Merlot NV, Tesco `14` `C`

Australian Red, Tesco `14.5` `B`

Australian Ruby Cabernet, Tesco `14` `C`

Australian Shiraz NV, Tesco `13` `C`

Australian Shiraz/Cabernet NV, Tesco `14` `C`

Barramundi Shiraz/Merlot NV `14` `C`

Best's Great Western Cabernet Sauvignon 1994 `14` `E`

Bleasdale Langhorne Creek Malbec 1997 `16` `D`

Wonderful warmth and richness. Very savoury and ripe but the thickness of the fruit is nigh spreadable on toast. Top 205 stores.

Brown Brothers Tarrango 1997 `15` `D`

Chapel Hill Coonawarra Cabernet Sauvignon 1996 `15.5` `E`

Cockatoo Ridge Grenache/Shiraz 1996 `15` `D`

Coonawarra Cabernet Sauvignon 1996, Tesco `15.5` `D`

Effortless lush, slightly minty, ripe red which would be wonderful with game dishes.

Cornerstone Grenache, Clare Valley 1997 `17` `E`

Magnificently aromatic plummy richness and softness and gorgeous Aussie sweaty warmth. A great treat for game dishes. Offensively modern, brash, full-frontal and unashamedly luscious. Top eighty-five stores.

Cranswick Estate Dry Country Cabernet Sauvignon 1996 `16` `D`

Terrific value here: a mature Aussie in prime condition. It's rich, dry, stylish, has fully integrated elements and motors like ruffled denim across the taste buds. Top eighty stores.

Geoff Merrill Cabernet Sauvignon Reserve 1994 `16` `E`

Lafite – eat your heart out. Grow cabbages – this wine is so delicious, woodily elegant, warm yet serious cabernet you wonder if pigs can fly after all. Top eighty stores.

Geoff Merrill Shiraz Reserve 1994 `18` `F`

A stunningly concentrated, smooth yet spicy shiraz of such depth, persistence and richness it puts many a Hermitage at four times the price to shame. A lovely fruity wine of great class. Top eighty stores.

Hardys Nottage Hill Cabernet Sauvignon/ Shiraz 1998 `16` `D`

Loads of savoury plums and blackberries with lovely earthy tannins. Scrumptious drinking here.

Kingston Estate Murray Valley Shiraz 1994 `14` `D`

Leasingham Classic Clare Shiraz 1995 `13.5` `G`

Too much! Too much fruit, too much money! Yes, it's lush and lovely with gorgeous tannins, but twenty quid's worth?! I think not. Top eighty-five stores.

Ninth Island Pinot Noir 1998 `13` `E`

Rosemount Estate Shiraz/Cabernet 1998 `15.5` `D`

So deliciously sweet and fruity: soft and full yet delicate on the finish. Deliciously approachable and warm.

Rosemount Shiraz 1998 `14.5` `E`

Very juicy and ripe and the tannins come late into it. With food? My choice would be lamb pasanda or imam biyaldi. At most stores.

St Hallett Cabernet Merlot 1996 `14` `E`

Bit juicy on the finish but jolly drinkable. Tannins have little grip, though. Top eighty-five stores.

St Hallett Faith Shiraz 1996 `13.5` `E`

Very gooey and adult-Ribena-ish for me. And at this price, shouldn't we expect more complexity, subtlety and guile? Top 200 stores.

Stonyfell Metala, Shiraz/Cabernet Sauvignon 1996 `11` `E`

I have never been able to enthuse about this medicinally labelled and quite ghoulishly juicy – rampantly so! – wine. It does indeed seem like a brew to restore iron in invalid nonagenarians. Top eighty-five stores.

Temple Bruer Cornucopia Grenache 1997 `14` `D`

Lovely spicy undertone. Not at all stores.

Temple Bruer Langhorne Creek
Shiraz/Malbec 1996 `16` `D`

My goodness! Talk about fruit juice with attitude! This wine seems so juicy at first, revealing every soft hedgerow fruit in a shameless degree of ripeness, but then it strikes tannically and characterfully on the throat. Top 205 stores.

AUSTRALIAN WINE WHITE

Australian Chardonnay, Tesco `16` `C`

Terrific value here, fully represented by the exuberance of the blue rollers on the label as much as by the tidal wave of flavour in the fruit. Lush, loving, warm, delicious.

Australian Colombard/Chardonnay, Tesco `13.5` `C`

Australian White NV, Tesco `14` `B`

Blues Point Semillon/Chardonnay 1998 `12.5` `D`

Not at all stores.

Brown Brothers Late Harvest Muscat 1997 `15.5` `D`

Try it as a daring aperitif. It's floral, gently honeyed and somewhat thick. It goes with light puddings – like raspberry fool – and it has some real ripe character to it which makes it quirkily different. Top 205 stores.

Chapel Hill Reserve Chardonnay 1996

Starts with a trumpeting richness, finishes clean with a high piccolo-like note of freshness. Top eighty-five stores.

De Bortoli Noble One 1994 (half bottle)

Quite gorgeous sweet wine which somehow contrives to offer honey, nuts and hard fruit in such off-burnt harmony that it surprises by its complexity and breadth of flavour rather than a full-frontal sweetness. This was one of the special Christmas '98 lines at Wine Advisor Stores only, so please note that stocks may be limited by now.

Geoff Merrill Chardonnay Reserve 1995

Delicious Le Montrachet style Aussie with all the thrilling vegetality that implies but no sullenness on the finish. A brilliant wine of great class and world-class winemaking. Top eighty stores.

Hardys Stamps of Australia Grenache/ Shiraz Rosé 1998

Good barbecue rosé. Not at all stores.

Jacobs Creek Dry Riesling 1998

Great with Chinese food, though this is not a spicy riesling at all so don't go barmy with the chillies. At most stores.

Lindemans Bin 65 Chardonnay 1998

Supremely sure of itself, this well-established brand showing, in its '98 manifestation, what a great year this is for Aussie whites from the region (Hunter Valley). This has great hints of warm fruit balanced by complex crispness and acidity. A lovely under-a-fiver bobby dazzler. Top 205 stores.

Lindemans Padthaway Chardonnay 1997 | 16 | E |

Smacks of fresh melon, pineapple and with a hint of toasted nuts with a touch of butterscotch. Enough for you? Top 205 stores.

Mount Pleasant Elizabeth Semillon 1994 | 15.5 | E |

Seems to be a rich beast as the aroma deliciously assaults the nostrils but then it strikes clean and fresh on the palate. Elegant and restrained – touch haughty even. Top eighty stores.

Ninth Island Chardonnay 1998 | 16 | E |

An expensive treat with its creamy depth and complex finish. Has a suggestion of old world vegetality but it is a triumph of cold fermentation and full fruit-retaining winemaking techniques.

Normans Unwooded Chardonnay 1998 | 16 | D |

It's as green and gracious as any Chablis from a great vintage and a beautiful vineyard.

Oxford Landing Sauvignon Blanc 1998 | 14 | C |

Amazingly fresh and cheeky for a warm climate sauvignon.

Pewsey Vale Rhine Riesling 1998 | 15.5 | D |

Something to drink now, with rich mineralised edge, or to cellar to anything up to five or seven years whereupon the real classic riesling attributes of petroleum and under-ripe melon will be more concentrated. It could rate 17 or 18 by the year 2005. Top 205 stores.

Rosemount Chardonnay 1998 | 15.5 | D |

Always one of Australia's most accomplished chardonnays. Class and composure, fluency and flavour. Available at most stores.

Rosemount Semillon/Sauvignon 1998 | 15.5 | D

A wine for complex fish dishes because it combines the fruity richness to combat the food plus the incisive edge of fine acids to refresh the palate and enhance the experience of food and wine between mouthfuls. Available at most stores.

Rymill Coonawarra Sauvignon Blanc 1997 | 15 | D

Smooth Voluptuous White NV, Tesco | 15 | C

Curiously the reverse of smooth and voluptuous. But this only adds to the tension. This is a charming, direct, gently fruity and very even-tempered wine.

St Hallett Poachers Blend 1997 (25cl) | 15 | A

Delicious little treat to enjoy with the same retailer's lunchtime snack offerings and sandwiches. Also available in 75cl. Top 200 stores.

Tasmanian Chardonnay 1998, Tesco | 16 | D

A rich, very rich, melon-edged chardonnay of impressive layered fruit but with a nice leavening of pert, pineapple acidity – very subtle but significant.

AUSTRIAN WINE RED

Blauer Zweigelt Lenz Moser 1997 | 16 | C

Brilliant! The best vintage yet for this Beaujolais of the Danube. Has more texture and soft richness but that unique smoked rubber and baked plum fruit is intact. Get chilled!

AUSTRIAN WINE WHITE

Lenz Moser's Prestige Beerenauslese 1995 (half bottle)

Delicious ripe honey, lemon peel, orange zest and melony ripeness as a subtle undertone. Great with fresh fruit or a creme brulee.

BULGARIAN WINE RED

Bulgarian Merlot Reserve 1994, Tesco

Very dry and arthritic-edged. Needs barbecued boar – bristles, tusks and all. At most stores.

Reka Valley Bulgarian Cabernet Sauvignon, Tesco

CHILEAN WINE RED

Altum Terra Mater Cabernet Sauvignon Reserve 1997

Terrific sweet-natured red for Indian food!! Not typical of Chile, and it's pricey. True, it has tannin, but the cherry and blackcurrant fruit is rich and glucoid.

Altum Terra Mater Merlot Reserve 1997

Very rich and earthy, pricey, untypical-of-Chile merlot. Wonderful with rich exotic food – like Balti stew – but the price? Difficult to swallow. Not at all stores.

Caballo Loco No 2, Valdivieso NV

Much better than the first release of this wine. The number two is more elegant and very impactful.

Canepa Zinfandel 1998

The tannins overexcite the fruit. Top twenty-five stores.

Chilean Cabernet Sauvignon NV, Tesco

Chilean Cabernet Sauvignon Reserve 1998, Tesco

Brilliant layered richness and brightness of fruit. Goes from juicy ripeness through rich fat tongue-lashing chocolate edginess, then turns on a subtle cocoa-and cassis edge. Fantastic drinking here.

Chilean Merlot Reserve 1998, Tesco

Shows the lovely subtle sweetness of young merlot, gentle yet gripping tannins, and well developed balanced fruit of some wit. Not at all stores.

Chilean Red NV, Tesco

Earthy and rich, it comes across more like a Tuscan red than one from Chile. As such, with the dryness and food versatility, this implies this wine is a highly drinkable bargain. At most stores.

Cono Sur Pinot Noir 1998

Plastic corked and otherwise not typical pinot either. It has some rich tannins for a start and the cherry undertone has to be searched for. But, as a solid red, it's absolutely fine. Top 200 stores.

Errazuriz Cabernet Sauvignon Reserve 1996

Finishes like a Pauillac, a Lynch-Bages say, of twelve years vintage (and a ripe warm vintage to boot). But this slight criticism (joke) is one's reward for permitting the taste buds to be so beautifully battered by the thick, rich, dark, savourily-tannic fruit. Like a Bordeaux, really. G. Archer is like L. Tolstoy by analogy but who would compare them in truth? Indulge me in my little extravagances. Top 200 stores.

Errazuriz Merlot El Descanso Estate 1997

Soft leather, cherries and blackberries and hints of earth, ripe yet cuddly tannins, and a rich, warm finish. An admirable merlot of class and cosiness. At most stores.

Errazuriz Syrah Reserva 1997

Ah! The poor Aussies . . . they knock the Frogs for six, then along come the Chileans with this opening bat. Life's a bitch isn't it guys?

Great With Indian 1997, Tesco

Isla Negra Cabernet Sauvignon 1997 16.5 C

With its plastic cork guaranteeing no taint, this is a perfect wine for the finely palated, for it is in perfect cabernet shape: rich, clinging, dry yet cassis-edged, very swirling and dark and all-engulfingly slurpable.

Luis Felipe Edwards Reserva Cabernet Sauvignon 1996

A cabernet lover's dream: tannic pertness, rich vegetal fruit with hints of green pepper and white pepper, balance, tenacity on the palate, and huge drinkability. One of the most classic Bordeaux style of Chilean cabs, it provides a smooth yet eventful ride. Not at all stores.

Montgras Merlot 1997

Utterly disgraceful! How is the honest wine snob, who regards under-a-fiver wines as anathema, to keep his prejudiced pecker up when he can spend £4.50 on a merlot as aromatic, textured and thrilling as this? The authorities should be alerted. About 200 stores.

Santa Ines Cabernet/Merlot 1997

The fruit is almost as black as its delicious taint-free plastic cork. It's rich and dry, deep and wonderfully energetic. Not at all stores.

Santa Ines Legado de Armida Cabernet Sauvignon Reserve 1997

Almost dainty, at first sip, then it turns ferociously eloquent and rich in the back of the gullet and shows great dry character and teeth-clenchingly classy tannins. Top eighty stores.

Santa Ines Malbec 1998

What great value here! It comes across with vivid but tasty tannins and such pertinacity of fruit that you wonder why malbec isn't as famous as cabernet sauvignon. This is a lovely savoury food wine of some class. Not at all stores.

Terra Mater Cabernet Sauvignon 1997 `13` `C`

A sweet innocent cabernet. Not at all stores.

Undurraga Carmenere Reserve 1997 `12` `D`

Too much, too ripe, too gawky. Top 200 stores.

**Undurraga Familia Cabernet Sauvignon
1995** `14` `E`

Very expensive and impressively rich and warmly textured. The tannins are impressive but I wish it were cheaper.

Undurraga Pinot Noir 1998 `14.5` `D`

Not classic pinot but immensely drinkable as a representative of dry, cherry/plum/blackberry ripe fruit with no hint of farmyard, true, but loads of personality.

**Valdivieso Chilean Cabernet Franc
Reserve 1996** `16` `E`

Classier than any Chinon, that's for sure. Top eighty-five stores.

Vitisterra Cabernet Sauvignon 1997 `15.5` `D`

Top 200 stores.

CHILEAN WINE   WHITE

**Canepa Wine Maker's Selection Oak Aged
Semillon 1997** `15` `C`

Chilean Chardonnay Reserve 1997, Tesco

Lovely depth of sophisticated unsnottiness here: dry, rich and deliciously melon and lemon ripe. Subtle yet forceful, calm yet enthusiastic.

Chilean Chardonnay, Tesco

Bit nervous on the finish, and only subtly suggestive of chardonnay in its rich and melon form, but drinkable enough.

Chilean Sauvignon Blanc NV, Tesco

Hints of grass to some fairly chewy fruit. Good for fish dishes, soups and salads.

Chilean White NV, Tesco

Great value tippling here. Not complex or intensely dry but has charming sotto-voce fruit.

Errazuriz Chardonnay 1997

I love the nutty, baked fruit aroma and the gentle fumaceous edge to the fruit as it descends, plump, ripe yet elegant, down the throat. Utterly delicious. About 400 stores.

Errazuriz Chardonnay Reserva 1996

Big edge to the keenly fresh fruit which gives it bulk. The creamy, smoky edge is very fine. Not a full wine, it's better mannered than that, but it has oodles of class. Top 205 stores.

Laura Hartwig Chardonnay 1997

From a bottle with a label which suggests the agonised auto-biography of a misunderstood ex-Public School headmistress, there emerges a gently woody and extremely engaging beauty of measured style. Wine Advisor Stores only.

Luis Felipe Edwards Chardonnay Reserve 1997 | 15.5 | C

The texture of the fruit is perfect here: ripe yet fresh, deep yet clean. Top eighty-five stores.

Santa Ines Sauvignon Blanc 1998 | 16.5 | C

Terrific value here. It has lovely texture, gently oily, and a lovely undertow of rich fruit pulling the acidity along in it wake. A better sauvignon than no end of overpriced Sancerres. Not at all stores.

Undurraga Chardonnay/Sauvignon Blanc 1998 | 15.5 | C

Undurraga Gewurztraminer 1998 | 13.5 | C

Interesting up front, but the finish seems to miss the mark and the elegance of the well-tailored materials finishes slightly raggedly. Top eighty-five stores.

ENGLISH WINE   WHITE

Chapel Down Summerhill Oaked NV | 12 | C

Three Choirs Estate Reserve Lightly Oaked 1996 | 12.5 | D

FRENCH WINE   RED

Baron de la Tour Fitou 1997   `14` `C`

Seems to be a conventional dry, herby, sunny Fitou as it lashes the buds but the throat gets a real fresh edge of peeled plum. Not at all stores.

Boisset Bourgogne Pinot Noir 1996   `12.5` `D`

Bourgueil 1995   `12` `C`

Buzet Cuvee 44 1997   `14.5` `C`

Chateau Clement Pichon, Cru Bourgeois
Haut Medoc 1996   `13` `G`

Classic cigar box aroma falls away into dryness and austerity on the finish. Probably needs five or six years yet. Top thirty stores.

Chateau de Cote de Montpezat, Cotes de
Castillon 1996   `15.5` `D`

Chateau Ginestiere Coteaux du Languedoc
1997   `15.5` `C`

A juicy modern wine but also full of character and dryness. A terrific price for such a gluggable wine.

Chateau Haut-Chaigneau Lalande de
Pomerol 1996   `14` `G`

Again, a '96 claret which needs years to come really good. In this case, three or four. Top thirty stores.

Chateau La Raze Beauvalet Medoc 1996 `13.5` `D`

Chateau la Tour de Mons Bordeaux 1996 `13.5` `G`

An expensive treat which will deepen in appeal if cellared for another five years. Top thirty stores.

Chateau Lafarque Pessac Leognan 1996 `12` `G`

Needs another seven or eight years. Top thirty stores.

**Chateau Liliane-Ladouys Cru Bourgeois
Superieur Saint-Estephe 1996** `12` `G`

The most immediately drinkable of Tesco's '96 clarets. But what dodgy value. Yes it's classy but Tesco has wines with more exciting fruit at a quarter of the price. Top thirty stores.

**Chateau Maucaillou, Cru Bourgeois Moulis
en Medoc 1996** `12` `H`

A nice £6's worth of fruit. Top thirty stores.

**Chateau Tour de l'Esperance Bordeaux
Superieur 1997** `16` `C`

Classic claret at an astonishing price. Has smoky richness, developed charcoal tannin, and the fruit, brave and battling, shines through. Top 200 stores.

Corbieres, Tesco `14.5` `B`

Cotes du Rhone, Tesco `13` `B`

Cotes du Rhone Villages 1997, Tesco `14.5` `C`

Domaine de la Grande Bellane Valreas Cotes du Rhone Villages 1997   16 D

Ragged yet dainty on its feet, this richly finishing, very dry wine combines a fair spread of hedgerow fruit and delicious tannin. It is classic Rhone Villages red. Great drunk out of a Viking horn or sipped with lievre a la royale. Top 200 stores.

Domaine de Lanestousse Madiran 1994   16 D

Oh yes! The tannin here is well held by the earthiness of the fruit – tobacco-scented and ripe – and the finish is rousing. Not at all stores.

Domaine Marguerite Carillon Volnay 1er Cru, Les Santenots 1996   12 G

Top eighty stores.

Four Corners Fine Cabernet/Merlot 1997   13.5 E

Top eighty stores.

Four Corners Fine Merlot 1997   13.5 E

Top eighty stores.

French Cabernet Sauvignon Reserve, Tesco   14 C

French Cabernet Sauvignon, Tesco   15.5 B

French Grenache Prestige, Tesco   14.5 C

Smells cabbagey but gets into terrific gear on the taste buds with food.

French Grenache, Tesco `14` `B`

French Merlot Reserve, Tesco `14.5` `C`

French Merlot VdP de la Haut de l'Aude, Tesco `15` `B`

Gamay, Tesco `10` `B`

Gevrey Chambertin 1997 `12` `G`

Top 200 stores.

La Bareille Beaujolais 1997 `10` `C`

La Vieille Ferme Cotes du Rhone 1996 `15.5` `C`

Delicious warm spicy stuff – fresh baked, rich and ready. Gorgeous tannin and quirkily-edged dry fruit.

Les Etoiles French Organic Red Wine NV `13` `C`

Earthiness is its most significant feature. Bit, though, like Cyrano's hooter – it tends to overshadow other aspects. Top 200 stores.

Les Fiefs de Lagrange, St Julian 1995 `16` `G`

Big and tannic and hugely chewy. A brilliant posh wine for the roast game. Top eighty-five stores only.

Louis Jadot Moulin a Vent 1996 `11` `E`

Minervois, Tesco `14` `B`

Nuits St Georges, Les Chezeaux 1996 `13` `G`

Has some tannins to the juice. Top eighty stores.

Oak Barrique Syrah 1995 `15` `D`

Pauillac 1994, Tesco `13` `D`

Pommard 1er Cru, Clos des Verger 1996 `13.5` `G`

Top 200 stores.

Savigny Les Beaune 1996 `11` `E`

St Emilion, Tesco `13` `D`

Syrah VdP d'Oc, Tesco `13.5` `B`

Terroir de Tuchan Fitou 1995 `14` `E`

Totally tastes of vinified hedgerow: sweet, earthy, brambly, delicious. Pricey, though.

Vintage Claret 1996, Tesco `15` `C`

FRENCH WINE   WHITE

Alsace Reserve La Pagode 1998 `12` `C`

Barrique Aged Marsanne Roussane 1997 `15.5` `C`

Seriously nutty, gently rich wine with a gooseberry heart, subtle but clinging, with a fruit and lemon finish. It provides an elegant and firmly fruity rebuke to the idea that the Languedoc is no producer of charming, uncluttered whites.

Cabernet de Saumur Rosé, Tesco `13.5` `C`

Chateau de la Grange Muscadet 1996 `12` `C`

Chenin Blanc, VdP du Jardin de la France, Tesco `15` `B`

Cotes du Rhone Blanc NV `14` `C`

Domaine de la Jalousie Late Harvest 1998 `14` `C`

A deliciously different, if sweetish, aperitif or wine for light fruit tarts. Not at all stores.

Domaine de la Jalousie VdP des Cotes de Gascogne 1998, Tesco `14.5` `C`

Nervous edge of chewy pineapple and overall a real thirst-quencher.

Domaine de Montauberon Marsanne 1998 `12` `C`

Not at all stores.

Domaine du Soleil Chardonnay VdP d'Oc NV (vegetarian & vegan) `15.5` `C`

Domaine du Soleil Sauvignon/Chardonnay NV (suitable for vegetarians & vegans) `14` `C`

Domaine Saubagnere, VdP des Cotes de Gascogne, Tesco `13.5` `C`

Entre Deux Mers, Tesco `13` `C`

Fait Accompli Rhone Valley 1997 `13` `C`

Four Corners Bordeaux Sauvignon Blanc 1997 14 C

Four Corners Chenin/Chardonnay 1997 13.5 C

French Chardonnay NV, Tesco 12 C

Touch raggedy on the finish.

Gaston d'Orleans Vouvray Demi Sec 1998 12 D

Not at all stores.

Great With Chinese Muscat/Sauvignon Blanc 1997, Tesco 13 C

James Herrick Chardonnay 1997 16 C

One of southern France's most accomplished, classically styled, bargain chardonnays.

La Cote Chery Condrieu 1996 13 G

Laperouse VdP d'Oc White 1995 15 C

Les Estoiles Organic Chardonnay/Chenin VdP d'Oc NV 13.5 C

Sticky rich yet appley. Has echoes, indeed, of Cox's Orange Pippin apple crumble.

Macon Blanc Villages 1998, Tesco 11 C

Not at all stores.

Meursault Louis Josse 1995 12 G

**Muscadet de Sevre et Maine Sur Lie
1997, Tesco** `13.5` `C`

Muscat de Rivesalte, Tesco (half bottle) `14.5` `B`

Premieres Cotes de Bordeaux, Tesco `13` `C`

**Puligny Montrachet Premier Cru 'La
Mouchere' 1996** `12` `H`

Sancerre 1998, Tesco `12` `E`

Saumur Blanc, Tesco `13` `C`

Sauvignon Gris Bordeaux 1997 `15.5` `D`

Most unusual level of Bordeaux fruit here: asparagus, grass,
lemon and chervil. Top eighty-five stores.

Vouvray, Tesco `13` `C`

White Burgundy 1998, Tesco `10` `C`

GERMAN WINE WHITE

Fire Mountain Riesling 1997 `13.5` `C`

Almost very good . . . but. Well, it should be £3.49 and there
needs to be a touch more fruit as the wine crisply attacks the
taste buds.

Liebfraumilch, Tesco `12` `B`

Nierstein Kabinett, Tesco   `12.5` `B`

Nierstein, Tesco   `13.5` `B`

St Johanner Abtey Spatlese 1995, Tesco   `13` `B`

**Steinweiler Kloster Liebfrauenberg
Kabinett, Tesco**   `13.5` `C`

**Steinweiler Kloster Liebfrauenberg
Spatlese, Tesco**   `12.5` `C`

Villa Baden Chasselas NV   `12` `C`

I find it as difficult to comprehend the ululating beast on the label as I do the howling fruit in the bottle. At most stores.

HUNGARIAN WINE   RED

Reka Valley Hungarian Merlot, Tesco   `13.5` `B`

HUNGARIAN WINE   WHITE

Chapel Hill Pinot Noir Rosé 1998   `15` `B`

A lovely cherry-edged but crisply finishing rosé of commendable elegance. Top 200 stores.

Hungarian Oak Aged Chardonnay, Tesco   `13` `C`

Reka Valley Hungarian Chardonnay, Tesco

Tokaiji Aszu 1990

Will age for ten to twelve years (and more) but it will go well with goose liver – which I drank it with. It lacks conventional sweetness but has a rich acidic vein like marmalade and lime. It was bought in specially for last Christmas at the top eighty-five stores, so please be aware that stocks may be low now.

ITALIAN WINE   RED

**Argiolas Cannonau di Sardegna 1996
(Sardinia)**   14   D

Barbera d'Asti Calissano 1997   15.5   C

**Barrique Aged Negroamaro del Salento
1995**   16   D

Real brilliance which southern Italy has made its own: a wine with figgy ripeness and raisiny richness yet with terrific compensating, earthy tannins. Top eighty-five stores only.

Chianti Colli Senesi 1997, Tesco   15   C

L'Arco Cabernet Franc, Friuli 1996   15.5   C

Merlot del Piave, Tesco   14   B

Merlot del Trentino, Tesco   15.5   C

Morellino di Scansano 1996

Pinot Noir del Veneto, Tesco

Sicilian Red, Tesco

Taruso Ripassato Valpolicella Valpentena 1997

Wild strawberry, cherries, licorice, almonds and sweet lushness overall. A wonderfully fruity wine of immense charm. It also has smooth tannins which will permit it to be aged for five or six years and become even lovelier (and perhaps reach 18/19 points). A superb food wine with such plumpness and depth it overrides the most robust food. Top eighty stores.

Tuscan Red, Tesco 14 C

Villa Pigna Cabernasco 1996

ITALIAN WINE WHITE

Alois Lageder Terlaner Sauvignon Blanc 1997

This makes out a good case for the grape but it is less exciting than New Zealand at the same price. It is, however, delicious, steely and crab-cake compatible. Top eighty-five stores.

Barbi Bianco di Custoza 1997

Touch bad value at £3.99 when Tesco has so many more virtuous bottles for less but this wine is nutty and crisp and comes alive with dead fish. Top eighty-five stores.

Elegant Crisp White 1998, Tesco　　15.5　C

A wine which lives up to its label billing! Great to sip, terrific with fish.

Frascati 1998, Tesco　　13　C

La Gioiosa Pinot Grigio 1998　　15　C

Comes in a patented thermic glass bottle which keeps the wine cooler, once removed from the fridge, for several hours. And the wine inside this modern marvel is well worth keeping. It's dry and deliciously apricot-edged.

Le Trulle Chardonnay del Salento 1996　　15　C

Le Trulle Dry Muscat 1998　　15.5　C

Wonderful summer aperitif. It's dry, as it promises, but the stealth of the smoky muscat fruit is delightful.

Orvieto Classico Abbocato 1998, Tesco　　14　C

Slid fruit, crisp on the finish, which would be perfect, for example, with spaghetti a la vongole.

Pinot Grigio/Chardonnay delle Venezie, Pasqua 1997　　14　C

Tuscan White, Tesco　　14.5　C

Most individual and attractively composed: nutty yet soft, fruity yet subtly vegetal.

Verdicchio Classico 1998, Tesco　　13.5　C

It's the price. Should be £3.29.

Villa del Borgo Pinot Grigio 1997 15.5 C

NEW ZEALAND WINE RED

Montana Reserve Merlot, Marlborough 1996 16 E

Superb balance of tannins and fruit: elegant, rich, dry, hints of spicy earth, a touch of chocolate. Lovely stuff.

New Zealand Cabernet Sauvignon NV, Tesco   13.5 C

NEW ZEALAND WINE WHITE

Azure Bay Chardonnay/Semillon 1998 11 C

Not at all stores.

Cooks Chardonnay, Gisborne 1998 13 D

Not at all stores.

Jackson Estate Sauvignon Blanc, Marlborough 1998 15.5 E

Ripe, fresh and plumply purposeful.

Kim Crawford Marlborough Sauvignon Blanc 1998   15.5   E

Very elegant and stylish. Dry but decisively fruity. Top eighty-five stores.

Lawsons Dry Hills Gewurztraminer 1998   16.5   E

Difficult trick pulled off here: can a gewurz be truly dry *and* full of vim? The answer with this delicious, aromatic, richly fruited specimen is a thunderingly fruity YES! Top eighty-five stores.

Montana Marlborough Riesling 1998   16   C

Interesting question: do you drink it now or keep it? Both are possible options. It has a lovely drinkable crispness and gentility of steely fruit but it will also age, over three or four years, with distinction and deepen in richness and complexity. Not at all stores.

Montana Reserve Chardonnay 1997   14.5   E

New Zealand Chardonnay, Tesco   15   C

New Zealand Dry White, Tesco   13.5   C

New Zealand Sauvignon Blanc 1997, Tesco   14   C

Rongopai Chardonnay Reserve 1996   16.5   E

A superbly wood chardonnay in the Montrachet mould. It only falls from the high standard, impeccable aroma and frontal fruit on the finish, which is quicker than a great wine would exhibit. This is, I feel, a function of its youth. But then if the acidity loses its grip – if one aged the wine for two more years – would the essential clean bite of the wine lessen? A conundrum – it is worth a tenner to try to solve it. Top eighty-five stores.

Stoneleigh Chardonnay 1997

Bite, vegetality, class and composure – true, it's not cheap. but that's NZ for you – bijou. Top 200 stores.

Villa Maria Private Bin Sauvignon Blanc 1998

Assured, elegant, crisp, a nigh perfect expression of sauvignon. It has firmness of purpose and balance of world class. Not at all stores.

Villa Maria Reserve Wairau Valley Sauvignon 1998

Keep it for eighteen months. Sure, it's lovely and elegant now but it will richly develop in bottle and possibly rate 17/18 points in a couple of years. Top eighty stores.

PORTUGUESE WINE RED

Alianca Particular Palmela 1995

Such sweetness and emulsion-thick texture yet it's dry, herby, very rich and classy on the finish. A terrific wine. Top eighty-five stores.

Bela Fonte Baga 1997

Terrific juicy fruit here. Delicious tarry richness and mature juiciness.

Bright Brothers Douro 1996

Very juicy and ripe yet, astonishingly, dry and tannic to finish.

Lovely trick to pull off here – great with food and for quaffing with serious company. Not at all stores.

Bright Brothers Old Vines 1996   14   C

Lush fruity charms – deep and delicious. Can be chilled and drunk with fish. Top eighty stores.

Dom Ferraz Bairrada 1997   16   C

Old Dom's back on form and sprightlier than ever! Terrific juice here – and serious underlying tannin. A tenacious wine of substance and style. Top eighty stores.

Dom Ferraz Dao 1997   16   C

Deeply layered and ripe, rich and flavoursome – loads of personality and pertinacity. Goes through a gamut of hedgerow fruit flavours and throws in a hint of licorice with lush tannin. A very accomplished piece of winemaking.

J P Barrel Selection Red Wine 1993   13.5   C

Very sweet follow-on from the previous vintage. Good with curries.

Palmela Particular 1995   16.5   D

Superbly well-muscled fruit here, hard-working, bold and vigorous and full of rich, concentrated, slightly jammy but not remotely soppy fruit. Has savouriness, texture, food-compatibility and is indeed particular (i.e. a.k.a. oddball).

Vinha Nova, Tras-os-Montes 1997   14   C

Cheap and utterly cheerful.

PORTUGUESE WINE WHITE

Bela Fonte Bical 1997

A meaty, nuttily rich wine of great appeal to anyone contemplating anything from Thai prawns to roast chicken. Top 200 stores.

ROMANIAN WINE RED

Four Corners Romanian Merlot 1998

Some dry fruit here which lacks a bit of punch on the finish.

Reka Valley Romanian Pinot Noir, Tesco

SOUTH AFRICAN WINE RED

Beyers Truter Pinotage NV, Tesco

Pinotage in its Sunday best. The tannins give it presence and persistence but there's none of the burnt rubber juiciness of the grape. Instead, we get well pressed and neatly pleated fruit of style and flavour.

Cape Cinsaut NV, Tesco

Cape Cinsaut/Pinotage NV, Tesco

Diemersdal Shiraz 1998

Interesting shiraz, at this price, more tobacco-scented, tannic complexity and ruffled-denim fruit than many an Aussie example of this grape for the same money. It finishes less sweetly than an Oz example, but its mid-palate performance, that is to say in the mouth and on the buds, is good and rich. Not at all stores.

Fairview Gamay Noir 1998

Goiya Glaan 1998 15.5 C

So much more exuberant, lively and charmingly fruity than any Beaujolais nouveau. Drink it for the sheer unpretentiousness of its immediate charm.

International Winemaker Cabernet Sauvignon/Merlot, Tesco 13 C

Kanonkop Paul Sauer 1994 15 G

Big and juicy and rather rumbustious. Great casserole red. Top twenty-two stores only.

Long Mountain Cabernet Sauvignon 1998

Very juicy and dry to finish. Not at all stores.

Oak Village Vintage Reserve 1997

Pinnacle Cabernet Sauvignon 1997

A deliciously tobacco-edged cabernet, not remotely shy, which turns in a serious smile of grim tannicity on the finish.

Pinnacle Merlot 1998

Yes, it's jammy and ripe but it has some lovely herby dryness underneath. Terrific quaffing here. Top eighty stores.

Plaisir de Merle Cabernet Sauvignon, Paarl 1995   `15.5` `E`

Robertson Cabernet Sauvignon 1997, Tesco   `15` `C`

Ryland's Grove Cinsault/Zinfandel 1997   `15` `C`

A light, gently spicy red of huge appeal.

South African Red, Tesco   `15` `B`

South African Reserve Cabernet Sauvignon 1996, Tesco   `15` `C`

Spice Route Andrew's Hope Merlot/ Cabernet, Malmesbury 1998   `16.5` `D`

The essence of new world cheekiness – it dares to be utterly unashamedly immediate and all-embracing. It's got so much jammy richness, which never goes gooey or blowsy. It's great, gorgeous and grandly underpriced. Top eighty stores.

Stellenbosch Merlot, Tesco   `15` `C`

Vergelegen Merlot 1995   `16` `E`

Exceedingly smooth yet rugged. Lovely merlot. Top eighty-five stores.

Woodlands Cabernet Sauvignon 1997   `15.5` `E`

SOUTH AFRICAN WINE   WHITE

Cape Chenin Blanc, Tesco   `14` `B`

Cape Colombar/Chardonnay, Tesco

Danie de Wet Green Label Chardonnay
1998

This has a high mark for such a subtle wine but this has nothing to do with the fact that its maker insists on paying for and sending me each month the Cape Wine magazine, but because it is trade mark chardonnay in its lovely balance of elements, restrained richness, calm and finesse. It doesn't grab you by the short and curlies, it has far too much stealth and wit for that.

Fairview Chardonnay 1997

Such deliciousness does not often come attached to such a reasonable benign price tag. It's wonderfully dry, classic, rich and very elegant. Nutty/fruity/vegetal – like a great minor white Burgundy in a fantastic year and an accident of low yielding vines and faultless winemaking dedication. Top eighty stores.

Great With Indian Colombard/Chardonnay
1997, Tesco

Oak Village Sauvignon Blanc 1998 [14] C

One of the richer styles of sauvignon, rather good with smoked fish dishes.

Paul Cluver Sauvignon Blanc 1997 [16] E

Steely, with a hint of crisp lettuce leaf but this is well coated with some textured fruit so the final effect is very, very classy. Top eighty-five stores.

Pinnacle Chenin Blanc 1997 [16] C

What an improvement since I first tasted it last autumn! Brilliant rich fruit hinting at dryness but so thick that the fruit, vegetal

and nutty with a lush edge, is very stylish, very high class chenin
and of an impactful generosity.

Plaisir de Merle Chardonnay 1996 `13` `E`

**Ryland's Grove Barrel Fermented Chenin
Blanc 1997** `15` `C`

Rylands Grove Sauvignon Blanc 1998 `15` `C`

Softly rich and ripe, rather classy and structured. Not hugely
fruity but nice gooseberry touches and solid refreshing qualities.
Neat finish.

**South African Chardonnay/Colombard,
Tesco** `14.5` `C`

**South African Reserve Chardonnay
1998, Tesco** `15` `C`

Delicious richness lapped by ripples of peaches/pineapple acidity.

South African White, Tesco `14` `B`

**Spice Route Long Walk Sauvignon
Blanc 1998** `16` `D`

Hint of earthy minerals and concentrated gooseberries. Excellent
structure and depth.

Vergelegen Chardonnay Reserve 1996 `16.5` `E`

A real Christmas treat. Has classic rotten-hay, melon and nutty
fruitiness, great aromatic presence, and a determined, very classy
finish. Top eighty-five stores.

SOUTH AMERICAN WINE   RED

Two Tribes Red   `13.5` `C`

SOUTH AMERICAN WINE   WHITE

Two Tribes White   `13.5` `C`

SPANISH WINE   RED

Berberana Dragon Tempranillo 1997   `14.5` `C`

Dry yet juicy, charred yet fleshy. Great little mouthful.

Bodegas Marco Real Garnacha Crianza, Navarra 1996   `16` `C`

Terrific food wine: soupy, dry, rich, full of vibrancy and mature fruit – and brilliantly lingering and ripely assertive. At most stores.

Don Darias NV   `15` `C`

Still keeping his nose in shape, this gent, and the Don has, in this latest blend, more tannins and ripe plummy fruit. He'll take you through a mild curry most charmingly.

Espiral Moristel Tempranillo/Cabernet Sauvignon 1998   `16` `C`

It's the blackcurrant jam richness which startles – but it's dry

and herby. Tannins and tenacity, style and utter drinkability –
a lovely wine.

Huge Red Juice 1998, Tesco

Wonderful stuff! It is hugely dry and juicy but this fruit is
classy and bouncy, like a young cru Beaujolais in a great year,
but there's the added tonic of rich tannins. A very versatile wine
– chilled with fish or meat or veg or cheese.

Marques de Chive Reserva 1994, Tesco

Can't imagine anything nicer with barbecued lamb chops or
Toulouse sausages. At most stores.

Marques de Grinon Rioja 1997

Not remotely typical. And this refreshing virtue makes it a Rioja
which can be both pleasurably gulped and drunk with all sorts
of food from risottos to grilled vegetables. Not at all stores.

Mendiani Tempranillo/Cabernet Sauvignon 1997

Light yet friskily flavoursome. Finishes in the throat more
robustly than its performance on the taste buds suggests. Not
at all stores.

Muruve Crianza 1996

Expensive but classy, ripe, rich and rivetingly fruity on the taste
buds. Top eighty stores.

Orobio Tempranillo Rioja 1997

Very fruity and not remotely over-woody or straining too hard.
Needs food.

Perdido Navarra Cabernet Sauvignon Crianza 1995

`16` `C`

Brilliant value here. The rich, textured, warmly tannic fruit has depth and weight and the polish has not obscured the character.

Piedmonte Merlot Tempranillo 1998

`14` `C`

Beaujolais lovers will lap it up!

Spanish Tempranillo 1996, Tesco

`13.5` `C`

Lovely rich beginning, bit of a sweet and soppy ending.

Valduero Ribera del Duero Crianza 1995

`15` `E`

A real treat – though a touch sweet on the finish – for it has lush tannins and forceful fruit.

Vina Mara Gran Reserva Rioja 1989, Tesco

`13.5` `E`

Too sweet for a tenner. Not at all stores.

Vina Mara Rioja Alavesa 1998, Tesco

`16` `D`

A simply terrific rioja. It just bounces with ripe, plump, dark fruit with lovely attendant tannins of savoury richness.

SPANISH WINE   WHITE

Agramont Cabernet Sauvignon Rosado 1998

`14` `C`

One of the crispest and cleverest of summer rosés. Top 200 stores.

Moscatel de Valencia, Tesco

URUGUAYAN WINE RED

Four Corners Tannat/Merlot 1998

Has a nice hint of the exotic. Very sunny and warm and richly welcoming. Top 200 stores.

URUGUAYAN WINE WHITE

Four Corners Sauvignon Blanc 1998

Crisp, clean and very spry. Top 200 stores.

USA WINE RED

Bonterra Cabernet Sauvignon 1996

Simply wonderful persistent fruit. It hammers home such brilliance of creamy richness and layered depth. It has great complexity and yet massive, scrumptious quaffability. A wonderful, immediate cabernet. Top 200 stores.

California Old Vine Estate Carignane 1996

Bit soupy.

California Old Vine Estate Zinfandel 1996   15   D

Fetzer Syrah 1996   16   E

Lovely dry richness under which beats a wild, soft heart of characterfulness. Available in Wine Advisor Stores only.

Fetzer Vineyards Private Collection Cabernet Sauvignon 1995   17   G

If you must spend fifteen quid on a cab style wine, then eschew Tesco's '96 clarets and go for this massively rich, sweet yet deeply serious, tannin-lush specimen. It reaches the levels of drinkability you can enjoy out of a spoon; who needs the convention of a glass? Wine Advisor Stores only.

Robert Mondavi Coastal Cabernet Sauvignon 1995   14   E

Very rich and tarry, more than a touch expensive for what it is, but hugely drinkable and enjoyable for those whose pocket is as deep as their throats.

Robert Mondavi Coastal Pinot Noir 1996   16.5   E

Smells of well-hung grouse and there's even a hint of truffle in there. The fruit is awesomely compacted and ripe compared with any Burgundy of the same price and the performance of the fruit as it rolls itself across the tongue is delightful. Classic pinot of personality and huge appeal to the pinot aficionado. A real treat.

Stratford California Zinfandel 1997   14.5   C

Tarry and rich and good with food.

USA WINE WHITE

Bonterra Chardonnay 1996 `17` `E`

Voluptuous! Yes, this wine is so – and it's rich, classy, sensual, deep, thought-provoking and utterly sinfully delicious. Top 200 stores.

Fetzer Barrel Select Chardonnay 1997 `14` `E`

Fetzer Viognier 1997 `16` `E`

Exuberant, spicy, richly elegant yet expressive of fun and roses, with gooseberries and apricots, this is a deliciously swirling, all-dancing viognier of great charm.

Stratford Chenin Blanc NV `14` `C`

A wine for Thai mussels – rich and spicy.

FORTIFIED WINE

---

10 Year Old Tawny Port, Tesco `13.5` `F`

Finest Madeira, Tesco `15.5` `E`

Mick Morris Rutherglen Liqueur Muscat (half bottle) `17` `C`

A miraculously richly textured pud wine of axle-grease texture and creamy figginess. Huge, world class.

**Superior Oloroso Seco Sherry, Tesco
(half bottle)** `15` `B`

**Superior Palo Cortado Sherry, Tesco
(half bottle)** `16.5` `C`

SPARKLING WINE/CHAMPAGNE

Asti NV, Tesco (Italian) `13` `C`

A real sweetie. Great-Great-Grandma, if she's remotely human,
will lap it up.

Australian Sparkling Wine, Tesco `14.5` `C`

Blanc de Blancs Champagne NV, Tesco `13.5` `G`

Not at all stores.

Blanc de Noirs Champagne NV, Tesco `14` `G`

Has some elegance and bite and that true suggestion of richness
which a Champagne made from black grapes can exhibit. Not
at all stores.

Cava, Tesco `16` `C`

Chapel Down Epoch Brut NV (England) `11` `D`

**Chapel Hill Sparkling Chardonnay
(Hungary)** `14.5` `C`

Dom Perignon 1990 　10　H

A commodity for rich people who have no palate, discrimination or common-sense. Top eighty-five stores.

Douglas Green Sparkling Brut NV (South Africa) 　10　E

I find it unconscionably dull and spiritless. Top eighty stores.

La Gioiosa Spumante Chardonnay/Pinot Noir 1998 (Italy) 　14　D

A charming little bubbly! Fresh as a spring daisy.

Laurent-Perrier Cuvee Rosé Brut NV 　11　H

Laurent-Perrier Vintage 1990 　13　H

Has some class but the price needs to go to Weight Watchers. Top eighty stores.

Lindauer Brut (New Zealand) 　13　E

Lindauer Special Reserve NV (New Zealand) 　14　E

Moet Vintage 1993 　13.5　H

Has some interesting fruit.

Mumm Cordon Rouge Cuvee Limite 1990 　12　H

Top eighty stores.

Mumm Grand Cordon 1990 　12　H

Hardly worth fifty quid of anyone's money.

Nicolas Feuillate Brut NV
13.5 G

Premier Cru Champagne Brut NV
15 F

Rosé Cava NV, Tesco
15.5 C

Deliciously dry and gently fruity, this classy specimen is the perfect summer bubbly. It makes many a much-vaunted Champagne blush to its roots at its price.

South African Sparkling Sauvignon Blanc 1998, Tesco
14.5 C

Taittinger Blanc de Blancs Comtes de Champagne 1989
10 H

Rip-off time. Top eighty stores.

Yalumba Pinot Noir Chardonnay
16 E

Yalumba Sparkling Cabernet Sauvignon NV
16 E

Tesco
Tesco House
PO Box 18
Delamare Road
Cheshunt EN8 9SL
Tel 01992 632222
Fax 01992 644235

WAITROSE

ARGENTINIAN WINE RED

Finca el Retiro Tempranillo, Mendoza 1998

Begins in a plum fresh vein, juicy and frisky, then turns deep and dark and moodily fruity. Lovely drinking.

Sierra Alta Cabernet Sauvignon/Malbec, Mendoza 1996

ARGENTINIAN WINE WHITE

La Bamba Mendoza Sauvignon Blanc 1998

Simple enough in its clean fruitiness but there's a subtle elegance too.

AUSTRALIAN WINE RED

Brown Brothers Barbera 1996

Interesting grape, barbera, for the full-rich-soft Aussie treatment. Italian in feel, yes, but Aussie in chutzpah.

Brown Brothers Tarrango 1998 12 D

Bushmans Crossing Grenache/Mataro 1998 `13` `C`

Bit too juicy and keen to be admired for me. But will chill well (in spite of its tannins).

Chateau Reynella Basket-Pressed Shiraz 1995 `17` `F`

Wonderfully rich beast of racehorse litheness with cart-horse endurance and muscle. It is highly aromatic, maturely fruity, deeply complex as it crushes all resistance from the taste buds, and the finish makes a much vaunted northern Rhone syrah seem positively jejune and spineless.

Fishermans Bend Cabernet Sauvignon 1998 `13.5` `C`

Jacob's Creek Grenache/Shiraz 1998 `14` `C`

Raunchy, restless and deeply engaging.

Nanya Vineyard Malbec/Ruby Cabernet 1998 `12` `C`

Penfolds Bin 2 Shiraz/Mourvedre 1997 `16` `D`

Alert, dry, ripe, firm, full of flavour and personality.

Penfolds Rawsons Retreat Cabernet Sauvignon/Shiraz/Ruby Cabernet 1997 `14` `D`

Again the princedom of soft manners sends out its rich, gooey ambassador.

Peter Lehmann The Barossa Shiraz 1997 `17.5` `D`

What a monster of Bacchic depravity! It would convert a celibate

nonagenarian teetotal nun to uninhibited acts of fruity aban-
don. Exciting and rich, hugely appealing and massively deep.

Rosemount Estate Cabernet Sauvignon
1998   15   E

Very juicy and ripe and with a lovely warm but subtle tannic
underbelly. It purrs like a cat.

Rosemount Estate Grenache/Shiraz 1997   13.5   D

The usual soft, soupy richness.

Rouge Homme Coonawarra Cabernet
Sauvignon 1994   13.5   E

St Hallet Gamekeepers Reserve, Barossa
1998   14   D

Smoky and dark.

Tatachilla Cabernet Sauvignon/Merlot 1997   16.5   E

A marvellous mouthful of baked herbs, tight tannins, rich fruit
and herby flavoursomeness of great depth.

Tatachilla Merlot, McLaren Vale 1996   14   E

Wynn's Coonawarra Michael Shiraz 1994   17.5   H

This has come on immeasurably in bottle since I first tasted it. It
is now one of the most deftly woven fruit-and-tannin Australians
I have ever tasted. It is intensely concentrated but very warm,
soft and aromatic, showing a cassis and toffee edge with the
texture, divine, of crimped velvet. A magnificent beast. It will
age with distinction but not beyond five or six years I believe
(contrary to the maker's ideas of longevity). It is the height
of luxury, this wine, for it has an impossibly smug hauteur and

sense of superiority. I love it. Available at Inner Cellar stores (0800 188884 for details).

Yaldara Reserve Grenache 1998 | 13.5 | D |

Very juicy and thickly textured. The Ribena school will love it.

Yarra Yering Pinot Noir 1991 | 12 | H |

AUSTRALIAN WINE WHITE

Basedow Barossa Chardonnay 1997 | 16 | E |

Such controlled lushness and complexity of acidity, it's excitement personified.

Bushmans Crossing Semillon/Chardonnay 1998 | 15 | C |

Great fish wine here but not one which can't be deeply agreeably sipped without food.

Cape Jaffa Unwooded Chardonnay 1998 | 16 | E |

A compellingly concentrated and most individual chardonnay of great untrammelled purity of fruit. Costs, but it delivers.

Chapel Hill Verdelho 1998 | 14 | E |

Needs Chinese food.

Chateau Tahbilk Marsanne, Victoria 1997 | 16 | D |

Love it! The sour-faced little puss!

Currawong Creek Chardonnay 1998

Superb gobbets of fat ripe fruit wreak havoc with the taste buds. Lovely oily fruit.

Hardys Stamp of Australia Grenache Shiraz Rosé 1998

Good barbecue rosé.

Houghton Classic Dry White 1998

Most accomplished blend: vigour, richness, texture, food versatility and real oomph here.

Leasingham Domain Clare Valley 1996

Gorgeous richness here with a hint of orange peel and lemon to the lovely thick melony fruit. Classy, warm yet fresh, deeply engaging.

Lindemans Winemaker's Reserve Padthaway Chardonnay 1995

A wine classier than many a Meursault at three times the price.

Nanya Vineyard Chenin/Gewurztraminer 1998

Brilliant value here: crisp, clean, subdued classy richness, and a zippy finish. Seriously amusing drinking.

Penfolds Clare Valley Organic Chardonnay/ Sauvignon Blanc, 1997

Always one of the Aussie's most elegant white constructs, this vintage shows even surer grip than previous ones.

Penfolds Koonunga Hill Chardonnay 1998 `16.5` `D`

What a great brand! Stunning richness and balanced, classy finish. If only white burgundians at three times the price could be this good.

Penfolds Rawsons Retreat Bin 202 Riesling 1998 `16` `C`

Puts riesling on a new plane at this price. Germany please copy!

Petaluma Piccadilly Chardonnay 1997 `17` `G`

So stiff with fruit, gelatinous, bold, emulsive, whipped like thick cream, that it seems the nearest thing to some sacred elixir.

Rosemount Estate Sauvignon Blanc 1998 `16` `D`

Why buy Sancerre when this beauty is the same price? It is lush yet lively, subtle yet rich. Terrific.

Rosemount Show Reserve Chardonnay 1997 `16` `E`

Such style and wit here. And it'll age for two or three years and grow more pointed.

St Hallett Semillon Select, Barossa Valley 1997 `17` `E`

Expensive treat which in its polished texture, complexity of fruit and fulsomeness of finish puts burgundies (which are chardonnays) costing five times more to shame.

Tatachilla Sauvignon Blanc/Semillon 1998 `14.5` `C`

Great chewy finish to some firm, well-packed fruit.

**Tea Tree Estate Colombard/Chardonnay
1998**

Knock-out value here: real rich yet balanced fruit.

BULGARIAN WINE — WHITE

**Domaine Boyar Premium Oak Chardonnay
1997**

Not remotely woody to my palate – and not rated on this basis
– I just like the incisive lemonic lushness.

CHILEAN WINE — RED

Concha y Toro Merlot 1998

Deliciously sweet and rich, if not typically merlot.

Cono Sur Cabernet Sauvignon, Rapel 1998

Unusually gruff-voiced, gravelly Chilean cabernet – but high
class and very accomplished.

**Isla Negra Cabernet Sauvignon, Rapel
1997** 17 C

Such unencumbered fruit! It's pure, rich, dry, exuberant yet very
classy. The texture is superb.

La Palmeria Merlot, Rapel 1998 `16.5` `C`

It combines that wonderful Chilean double-whammy of food fitness and great, concentrated, complex drinking. Gorgeous stuff.

La Palmeria Reserve Merlot, Rapel 1998 `17` `D`

Words fail me. The wine won't let me describe it. I can manage the figure 17-points but my wrist, numb with leathery fruit coursing down my arteries, will not further flicker.

Santa Rita 120 Cabernet Sauvignon, Maipo 1997 `16` `C`

Gorgeous woody dryness and richly textured, bargain fruit.

CHILEAN WINE WHITE

Conch y Toro Sauvignon Blanc 1998 `16` `C`

Simply so much better textured and opulent than Sancerre and more impishly gooseberryish and grassy.

San Andres Sauvignon Blanc, Lontue 1997 `14.5` `C`

ENGLISH WINE WHITE

Bacchus 1996 `11` `C`

Grassy and muddy. Not, though, a wine I can admire.

Chapel Down Summerhill Oaked Dry White 11 C

Denbies Surrey Gold 12 C

FRENCH WINE RED

Boulder Creek Red VdP du Vaucluse 1998 14 B

A simply delicious wine, great chilled, for fish, meat and vegetable barbecues.

Chateau Cazal-Viel, Cuvee des Fees St Chinian 1998 16 D

Ripe, plump and completely sure of itself. Wonderful stuff.

Chateau de Jacques Moulin a Vent 1997 12 E

Chateau Haut d'Allard Cotes de Bourg 1997 15 D

An incredibly smooth claret of quite startling fatness yet youth.

Chateau Le Tertre Bordeaux 1996 14 C

Chateau Pech-Latt, Corbieres 1997 16.5   C

Superb fruit here – beautifully concentrated and warmly welcoming. Lovely ripe finish – yet it's seriously deep and even a touch dandified.

Chateau Troplong Mondot, St Emilion Grand Cru Classe 1994 12 H

Magnificent tannins here. I'd blend it with a cheap Chilean merlot to bolster the fruit.

Cotes de Roussillon 1998

Richer and juicier version of the Minervois but still lovely and dry on the finish.

Cotes du Rhone 1998, Waitrose

Terrific value tippling here. Great for barbecues.

Cotes du Rhone Villages, Domaine de Cantemerle 1997

Deeply smooth and plumply mouth-filling. Lovely polish, great fruit and finely wrought, gentle tannins. Terrific stuff.

Cotes du Ventoux 1998

Cuvee-Eugenie Chateau Capendu, Corbieres 1997

Ten quid for a Corbieres? Oh yes – when it's better than many a £30 Hermitage. Wonderful texture, perfume and complex finish. An immensely classy wine which even manages to out-box many a much vaunted Aussie shiraz. Thus it is great value.

Domaine du Moulin 'The Cabernets', VdP d'Oc 1998

A marvellously dry and richly tannic, excitingly one-in-the-eye for claret blend of consummate drinkability and food versatility.

Fitou Mont Tauch 1997

Ripe plums, Gauloises, and juicy cherries, with a dry undertone.

**Fortant de France Grenache VdP d'Oc
1997**

Gevrey Chambertin Chauvenet 1996

Waitrose's best red Burgundy. Has some guts to it.

Good Ordinary Claret Bordeaux, Waitrose

Sweeter and richer than previous manifestations.

**L'Enclos Domeque Mourvedre Syrah VdP
d'Oc 1997**

A river of smoothly running, rich, deep fruit full of textured
interest.

La Colombe Organic Cotes du Rhone 1997

**Le Faisan Syrah Grenache VdP du
Gard 1998**

Can you imagine a wine pressed by old leathery souls (and soles),
crushed Cuban cigars, hedgerows of ripe blackberries and a pile
of herbs? No? Taste this wine!

**Les Fontanelles Merlot/Syrah VdP
d'Oc 1998** 16 C

Wonderful coming together of Hermitage and St Emilion –
Hermilion, shall we say? – in that the grapes, and the style
of the wine, of these two proud plots of vine and soil give
definite characteristic fruitiness here joined together in glorious,
good value fruit. Wonderful balance to the wine: dry/earthy,
fruity/layered, fresh/mature. A triumph for vin de pays rules
and New Worldliness.

Maury, Les Vignerons du Val d'Orbieu NV `16` `C`

A sweet red wine for chocolate-based puddings. Did I say sweet?
It hardly does this complex wine justice.

Merlot/Cabernet Sauvignon, VdP d'Aigues 1998 `15.5` `B`

Lovely fruit, tannins, herbs and a dry, lingering finish. Considerable class here.

Minervois 1998 `15.5` `B`

Herby, dry, seriously fruity, great tannins – has personality and
purpose.

Red Burgundy Pinot Noir JC Boisset 1996 `13` `D`

Saint Roche VdP du Gard 1998 (organic) `15.5` `C`

An organic wine of great dryness and richness. Has terrific
tannin.

Saumur Rouge Les Nivieres 1998 `14.5` `C`

Cherries and wild raspberries and rich tannin. Not as dry as
some, it'll take marvellously to chilling for summer thirsts.

Savigny les Beaunes Cave des Hautes-Cotes 1996 `11` `F`

Vin de Pays de l'Herault Tempranillo Syrah 1998 `16` `C`

Very plump fruit handsomely riddled with dry tannins. Has a
sense of fun with a deep, rich sensuousness.

Winter Hill Merlot/Grenache, VdP d'Oc 1998 `15` `B`

Very dry and richly characterful. Not a pussycat at all. But it still purrs.

Winter Hill Pinot Noir/Merlot VdP d'Oc 1998 `14` `C`

Oddly charming marriage which will progressively enrich itself for eighteen months.

Winter Hill Reserve Shiraz VdP d'Oc 1997 `15.5` `C`

Exceptional shiraz for the money which might send a shiver of apprehension up the spine of any Aussie (whose shiraz costs twice this one).

FRENCH WINE WHITE

Alsace Gewurztraminer 1997, Waitrose `16` `D`

Oh yes! This is a terrifically well-textured, spicy food wine. Wonderful surge of flavour, floral yet dry, on the finish.

Alsace Pinot Blanc, Paul Blanck 1997 `14.5` `C`

Great fruit here for an often plodding grape. Chewy and rich.

Anjou Blanc 1998 `12` `B`

Bergerac Blanc Marquis de Beausoleil 1998 `14.5` `B`

Great value here to make any well-charred fish go down more swimmingly.

331

Bordeaux Blanc Medium Dry, Yvon Mau

Chablis Grand Cru Blanchots, La Chablisienne 1995

Chardonnay VdP du Jardin de la France 1998

Terrific value. Has sour-melon richness and crispness beneath.

Chateau Liot Sauternes 1996 (half bottle)

Gorgeous marmalade thick waxy texture.

Chateau Terres Douces, Bordeaux 1996

Don't like its raw woodiness much.

Chateau Vignal Labrie, Monbazillac 1996

Dare you be this different and serve this as an aperitif instead of with the foie gras? It's honeyed and oily, not remotely sickly sweet but even a touch dry and vegetal on the finish. A wonderful individual wine of huge class for the money. It is not a dessert Monbazillac at all. It is the entrance to heaven – no: the exit.

Colombard Sauvignon Blanc, Comte Tolosan 1998

Terrific fruit here with even a hint of sauvignon seriousness to it.

Cuckoo Hill Chardonnay/Viognier VdP d'Oc 1998

What a scrumptious blend of two forcefully characterful grapes! Has spice, bite, smoothness and real wit.

**Domaine de Planterieu VdP de Gascogne
1998**

Daintily trips down the throat tasting of pears and pineapples.

**Gewurztraminer Alsace Les Princes Abbes
Domaines, Schlumberger 1995**

Not your all-in-yer-face spiciness but an elegance and ripeness
of deft charms. Inner Cellar stores.

**L'Enclos Domeque Barrel Fermented
Marsanne/Roussanne VdP d'Oc 1998**

A fine Rhone blanc taste-alike which will be wonderful paired
with river fish – trout, for example.

Le Pujalet VdP du Gers 1998

A pleasant aperitif tipple for back gardens in summer.

**Les Fleurs Chardonnay/Sauvignon VdP des
Cotes de Gascogne 1998**

Rather fat at first but then shows an astonishing litheness and
freshness as it quits the throat. A bold wine of individuality
and style.

**Muscat de Rivesaltes, M. Chapoutier 1996
(half bottle)**

**Muscate de Beaumes de Venise NV
(half bottle)**

Superb half bottle of riches and rampantly buttery sweetness.
Great for creme brulees, summer puddings and fools.

Rosé d'Anjou 1998, Waitrose

Stickily rich and great for barbecued foods.

Roussanne VdP d'Oc Ryman 1997

Subtle charms with a coating of fruit over some rather classy fresh acids. Lovely restraint.

Saint Roche Blanc VdP du Gard 1998

Most stylishly dry and deft. Accomplished level of blending which totally transcends the usual level of such grapes.

Saint-Aubin Premier Cru Ropiteau 1997

This is a wonderful anachronism: an expensive reminiscence of sullen vegetality and disappointed ducal hopes which recall Lear's 'waterish Burgundy' but also prompts the reflection that in five years' of ageing this wine might have legs.

Sauvignon Blanc 'Les Rochers', VdP des Cotes de Gascogne 1998

Wonderful texture, polished fruit, complex interplay of elements and purposeful finish.

Sauvignon de St Bris 1997

Delicious country classic of more engaging vegetality and fineness of fruit than most Sancerres.

Tokay Pinot Gris Vendanges Tardives, Hugel 1990

Butterscotch richness yet calm acidic complexity. A stunning aperitif wine. Inner Cellar stores.

Vin Blanc Sec VdT Francais NV, Waitrose

White Burgundy, Boisset 1996

**Winter Hill Reserve Chardonnay VdP
d'Oc 1998**

I'd rather touch it than a thousand rancid Mersaults. Real
class here.

Winter Hill Syrah Rosé, VdP d'Oc 1998

Great charm for picnics.

Winter Hill VdP de l'Aude 1998 14.5 B

Has a terrific chewy edge to it.

GERMAN WINE WHITE

**Avelsbacher Hammerstein Riesling
Auslese, Staatsweingut 1989**

**Graacher Himmelreich Riesling Spatlese,
JJ Prum 1994** 12 G

**Kiedricher Grafenberg Riesling Spatlese,
Rheingau 1989** 16.5 C

Yes, of course it's for serious drinkers only. People who cycle (but
love petrol); people who chewed coal when an infant; people who
like the feel of a wine which seems as if it really was pulled from

the bowels of the rich soil. An astounding bargain. The German bargain of the year.

Langenbach Riesling 1997 `13` `C`

Ockfener Bockstein Riesling QbA, Dr Wagner 1997 `13` `D`

Riesling Kabinett, Robert Weil 1996 `12` `E`

Ruppertsberg Riesling, Rheinpfalz 1996 `14` `C`

The every-day-sipping Nietzsche.

Villa Eden Liebfraumilch Rheinhessen 1998 `14` `B`

As good as a £3 Lieb can get.

HUNGARIAN WINE RED

Chapel Hill Cabernet Sauvignon Barrique Aged 1997 `C`

Superb blackcurrant dryness and herb-encrusted richness. Dry but delicious.

Deer Leap Dry Red Blauer Zweigelt 1997

Superb youth, suppleness, cherry/plum fruit, hint of tannin, ripeness and a touch of passion. Brilliant! Knocks Beaujolais for several sixes.

HUNGARIAN WINE WHITE

Chapel Hill Irsai Oliver, Balatonboglar 1998 | 13 | C

Deer Leap Chardonnay/Pinot Grigio 1998 | 14 | C
Delightful fish wine.

Deer Leap Gewurztraminer, Mor 1998 | 13.5 | C
Most effective with light Cantonese food.

Nagyrede Barrel Fermented Chardonnay 1996 | 13.5 | C

Nagyrede Cabernet Sauvignon Rosé 1998 | 12 | B

Tokaji Aszu 5 Puttonyos 1990 (50cl) | 16 | E
Great dessert richness.

ITALIAN WINE RED

Basilium Alta Vigna Merlot & Cabernet Basilicata 1998 | 16.5 | C

Superb multi-layered richness which proceeds in deliciously textured layers as it courses over the taste buds. Compelling wine.

Cent'are di Sicilia, Duca di Castelmonte 1997 | 15 | C

Individual in taste and texture and splendidly robustly fruity in defence of this singular outlook.

Chianti 1997, Waitrose `14` `C`

Dry and terracotta fruited.

Chianti Classico, Rocca di Castagnoli 1997 `16` `E`

Splendid old-fashioned but modern paradox. A real dinner party wine.

Chianti Colli Senesi 1997 (organic) `14` `D`

Touch expensive but the fruit has some elegance to it.

Montepulciano d'Abruzzo, Umani Ronchi 1997

Wonderful cheroot-scented fruit with great hedgerow richness and firm tannins. Brilliant.

Nero d'Avola/Syrah 1997 (Sicily) `15.5` `C`

Vivacity, impudence, raffish humanitarian character. Loveable rogue of an edge to it.

Poggio a'Frati Chianti Classico Riserva 1993

Those who say Chianti is old-hat should chew on this wine. Combines the swagger of a sombrero with the dusty seriousness of a bowler.

Primitivo Merum 1997 `16` `C`

Wonderful cherry/plum fruit, hint of craggy tannicity on the finish, and a full, free-flowing delivery of richness and depth.

Sangiovese Marche 1998, Waitrose

Cherry-ripe and earthy. The old Italian food-wine trick.

Teroldego Rotaliano, Ca'Vit 1997 | 16 | C

Gorgeous ripe texture, plump and cherry/blackcurrant deep. Very polished but far from all surface.

Terra Viva Merlot del Veneto 1998 | 13.5 | C

Very juicy.

Terre del Sole VdT Rosso (Sardinia) | 15.5 | C

Deliciously quirky, savoury, herby fruit.

Vino Nobile di Montepulciano, Avignonesi 1995 | 15 | E

Runs fluently over the taste buds leaving behind a herby residue.

ITALIAN WINE WHITE

Chardonnay MezzoMondo 1997 | 15 | C

Has great restrained melon richness, dryness and depth.

Moscato d'Asti, Villa Lanata 1997 | 16 | C

Wonderful honeyed, spicy, floral aperitif. Be different! Drink it with the in-laws!

Pinot Grigio Alto Adige, St Michael-Eppan 1997 | 13 | D

Soave Classico, Vigneto Colombara 1997

Superbly cool class and sophistication here. Strikes the palate with huge style. Possibly replaced by the '98 vintage by the time this book comes out.

Trebbiano Marche 1998, Waitrose

Superb texture and ripe fruit. Most unusually concentrated trebbiano.

Verdicchio dei Castelli Jesi, Moncaro 1998

Lovely rich, nutty fruit, ripe and deep, and deliciously balancing acidity. A most beautifully balanced specimen.

MEXICAN WINE RED

L A Cetto Petite Syrah 1996

Terrific value here. Has rich plum and blackcurrant fruit, lovely mature tannins and a good gentle wallop on the finish. Great stuff!

MOROCCAN WINE RED

Le Palmier Merlot/Cabernet Sauvignon 1997

Easily the most elegant, polished and vegetally complex Moroccan red I've tasted. Astonishing fleet-of-foot fruit.

NEW ZEALAND WINE RED

Church Road Reserve Cabernet Sauvignon/Merlot 1995

`15` `F`

Pricey and accomplished. Wonderful tannins on the finish.

Church Road Reserve Merlot, Hawkes Bay 1995

`13` `F`

Villa Maria Cellar Selection Cabernet/ Merlot, Hawkes Bay 1996

`14` `E`

I'd let it age in a dark underground room for another eighteen months or maybe two years.

NEW ZEALAND WINE WHITE

Jackson Estate Sauvignon Blanc, Marlborough 1998

`15.5` `E`

Ripe, fresh and plumply purposeful.

Tiki Ridge 1998

`14` `C`

Rippling with rich fruit, not subtle but it has some freshness.

Villa Maria Private Bin Chardonnay, Gisborne 1998

`14` `D`

Villa Maria Private Bin Riesling, Marlborough 1998   `15` `C`

A deliciously subtle and not entirely typical riesling. It will age for a couple of years with distinction and achieve weight and interest.

PORTUGUESE WINE   RED

Sinfonia Alentejo 1997   `16.5` `C`

The sheer polish of this wine as taste-bud-tinglingly rich and well textured. Superb fruit of great class for the money.

Terra de Lobos, Quinta do Casal Branco 1998   `16` `C`

Wonderful richness here, dry (and wry) complexity, earthiness, herbiness, tannins and lovely tenacity on the finish.

Vila Santa Alentejo 1997   `17` `E`

Magnificent classiness from colour through to aroma, fruit in the mouth to finish in the throat. Masterly performer.

PORTUGUESE WINE   WHITE

Quinta de Simaens Vinho Verde 1998   `10` `C`

Terras do Rio Quinta de Abrigada 1998   `15` `B`

Terrific value for fish barbecues here.

ROMANIAN WINE RED

River Route Limited Edition Merlot 1997

Rather claret-like in its dryness but it has a hint of Romanian sun and a hint of spice. Great food wine.

Willow Ridge Merlot/Cabernet (Oaked) 1997

Very juicy and fruity but the hint of wry character gives it charm.

Willow Ridge Pinot Noir 1998

Dry, touch earthy, nicely textured, rich, deep and very accomplished. Terrific blend of grapes.

SOUTH AFRICAN WINE RED

Avontuur Pinotage 1997

Clos Malverne Pinotage, Stellenbosch 1998

Always makes out a case for itself as the Cape's most feline pinotage.

Devon View Cabernet Sauvignon, Stellenbosch 1997 13.5 D

Fairview Malbec, Paarl 1997 16 D

Simply sings along – the fruit is compulsively quaffable.

Kumala Reserve Cabernet Sauvignon 1997   17   E

Wonderful one-off marvel of sublime cabernet class: pepper, cheroots, blackberries, tannins – it's got the lot. Plus superb textured richness.

Long Mountain Merlot/Shiraz 1997   13.5   C

Spice Route Andrew's Hope Merlot/Cabernet, Malmesbury 1998   16.5   D

What rivetingly rich, dark fruit. Compellingly well textured and the tannin/fruit harness is superb.

Steenberg Merlot, Constantia 1997   13   E

Minty and sweet.

Warwick Estate Old Bush Vine Pinotage, Stellenbosch 1996   15.5   E

SOUTH AFRICAN WINE   WHITE

Culemborg Unwooded Chardonnay, Western Cape 1998   13   C

Fairview Barrel Fermented Chenin Blanc 1998   17   C

God, I love this wine. What value for under a fiver. It simply screams with richness and style.

Jordan Chardonnay, Stellenbosch 1997

Big chewy white burgundy taste-alike. Great wine for chicken and posh seafood dishes.

Long Mountain Colombard/Riesling 1998

Chirpily cheeky and fresh.

Mission Vale Bouchard-Finlayson
Chardonnay Reserve 1997

Bit gawky for twelve pounds. Inner Cellar branches.

Robert's Rock Oaked Chardonnay 1998

Fabulous value. You can't quite believe fruit so proud and rich can cost under four quid.

Spice Route Abbotsdale Colombard/
Chenin Blanc 1998

What lovely clashing of flavours here. It is spritely yet richly and deeply drinkable. Remarkable balance and style.

Springfield Sauvignon Blanc Special
Cuvee 1998

A very classy Sancerre in style, but not price. It's superb.

Steenberg Sauvignon Blanc 1998

Chewy and grassy. Great with shellfish. Better than many a Sancerre.

Warwick Estate Chardonnay, Stellenbosch
1998

Superb balance of rich elements and the impressive vegetality and texture is better than almost all Montrachets at umpteen times the price. This is an astonishing bargain. Inner Cellar branches.

SPANISH WINE RED

Agramont Tempranillo/Cabernet Sauvignon, Navarra 1996

Has hints of tobacco, tea-leaf and blackcurrants (with a suggestion of earthy spiciness). It's robust, dry yet richly fruity, complex and bold. Concentrated and calm, classy and complete.

Albacora Tempranillo 1997

What is the remarkable thing is the sheer satiny texture which is beautifully crumpled with tannins.

Espiral Tempranillo/Cabernet Sauvignon 1997

Terrific thick fruit, spreadable on morning toast. Love it!

Navajas Rioja 1996

Creamy vanilla-edged fruit of great charm and persistence.

Totally Tinto Tempranillo, La Mancha NV

Terrific energy and richness here. Great price for such warm hearted fruit.

Vina Fuerte Garnacha, Calatayud 1998

What a lot of life this dry but pertly fruity wine provides. Adventurous, dry, food-friendly.

SPANISH WINE   WHITE

Clearly Blanco Penedes NV   `14` `B`

Summer feast wine. Real character and bite.

Espiral Macabeo/Chardonnay 1998   `13.5` `C`

Las Lomas Moscatel de Valencia   `16` `C`

Superb.

Vinas del Vero Chardonnay 1997   `16` `C`

Thunderingly gorgeous (subtle!) bargain. Wonderful grip. Great
style on the finish.

USA WINE   RED

**Bonterra Cabernet Sauvignon 1996
(organic)**   `17` `E`

Wonderful herby, sweet/dry fruit I defy even a Venusian not
to find totally drinkable.

**Fetzer Valley Oaks Cabernet Sauvignon
1996**   `16.5` `D`

Warm, all-embracing, deep, broad, and most charmingly well-
textured and ripe on the finish.

Redwood Trail Pinot Noir 1997   `14` `D`

Cherries and soft raspberry-edged fruit with a hint of tannin.
Better than a thousand Nuits St Georges.

Stone Bridge Cellars Zinfandel 1996   `15` `C`

The zin in playful, everyday quaffing mode.

Yorkville Cellars Cabernet Franc 1996 (organic)   `13` `E`

Very sweet.

USA WINE   WHITE

Bonterra Chardonnay 1996   `17` `E`

Deeply serious. No joking. This is better than M. Poubelle's Montrachet.

Edna Valley Vineyard Paragon Chardonnay 1996   `16` `F`

It joshes a bit, then turns seriously complex. Lingering woody finish of subtle charms. Inner Cellar stores.

Fetzer Sundial Chardonnay 1996   `14.5` `D`

Fetzer Viognier 1997   `15.5` `E`

Pebble dash fruit, gently chewy and full of flavour. Hint of dry apricot and nuts. Inner Cellar stores.

Redwood Trail Chardonnay 1996   `15.5` `D`

Redwood Trail Zinfandel Blush NV   `10` `C`

I hate pink zinfandel. It should be outlawed.

FORTIFIED WINE

10 Year Old Tawny, Waitrose   `14` `F`

**Apostoles Palo Cortado Oloroso
(half bottle)**   `15.5` `E`

Comte de Lafont Pineau des Charentes   `15` `D`

Dow's 1977   `16` `H`

Dry Fly Amontillado   `12` `D`

Fino, Waitrose   `15.5` `C`

Fonseca Traditional LBV 1983   `15` `G`

**Gonsalez Byass Matusalem Oloroso Dulce
Muy Viejo (half bottle)**   `16` `E`

The ultimate Everest for the taste buds. Can they climb the
peaks of this hugely rich, fruity, acidic, bursting-with-flavour
sherry? Or will they wilt?

Harveys Isis Pale Cream Sherry   `13` `D`

Jerezana Dry Amontillado, Waitrose   `16` `D`

A wonderful cold weather cockle warmer. Not remotely austere
or molly-coddley fruity, it's simply blood arousing.

Oloroso Sherry, Waitrose   `13` `C`

349

Pando Fino, Williams and Humbert `14.5` `D`

Rich Cream Sherry, Waitrose `13` `D`

Solera Jerezana Dry Oloroso, Waitrose `16.5` `D`

Fabulous chilled as an aperitif. Dry toffee fruit with a hint of almond.

Southbrook Farm's Framboise (half bottle) `15` `E`

Vintage Warre Quinta da Cavadinha 1986 `17` `G`

Gorgeous ripeness yet hugely concentrated acid and tannin, compacted and fully ameliorated, so that the final texture is magnificent.

White Jerepigo 1979 (South Africa) `14` `D`

SPARKLING WINE/CHAMPAGNE

Alexandre Bonnet Brut Rosé NV (France) `12` `G`

Brut Vintage 1990, Waitrose `13` `G`

Ah! A touch disappointing for eighteen smackers.

Canard Duchene Brut NV `12.5` `G`

Cava Brut NV, Waitrose `16` `C`

Quite superb.

Champagne Blanc de Blancs NV, Waitrose [15] [G]

Another brilliant example of Waitrose's superior Champagne buying skills. Other large retailers please copy!

Champagne Blanc de Noirs NV, Waitrose [15] [F]

The real thing. A fine champagne for the money.

Champagne Brut NV, Waitrose [12.5] [G]

Toasty and delicious. Has genuine depth of feeling and style. Real class here.

Charles Heidsieck Reserve Mise en Cave en 1993 [13.5] [H]

Clairette de Die Tradition (half bottle) (France) [14] [D]

Conde de Caralt Cava Brut NV [16.5] [D]

As elegantly labelled as the superbly polished fruit in the bottle.

Cremant de Bourgogne Blanc de Noirs, Lugny [14] [D]

Cremant de Bourgogne Rosé NV (France) [15] [E]

Better than many a Champagne.

Cuvee 2000 Champagne, Waitrose [18] [H]

Still tasting wonderful. A textbook blending exercise. Far better than many legends.

Cuvee Royale Blanquette de Limoux NV `13.5` `D`

Green Point Vineyards Brut, 1995 (Australia) `15` `F`

Rather haughty in its richness and grand champagne-style maturity.

Jacob's Creek Sparkling Chardonnay/Pinot Noir NV (Australia) `15` `D`

Great value.

Lindauer Brut (New Zealand) `14.5` `E`

Expressive of nothing but great value for money and utterly charming sipping.

Quartet NV, Roederer Estate (California) `14` `G`

Saumur Brut NV, Waitrose `14` `D`

Dry and decisive. Delicious!

Seaview Brut Rosé `14` `D`

Delicate little rosé.

Seaview Pinot Noir/Chardonnay 1995 (Australia) `16` `E`

Gorgeous, elegant stuff. Real class here.

Seppelt Great Western Brut (Australia) `13.5` `D`

Waitrose Limited
Southern Industrial Area
Bracknell
Berks RG12 8YA
Tel 0800 188884 (Customer service)
Tel 0800 188881 (Direct mail sales)

COMING SOON:

STREETPLONK 2000

Gluck's guide to High Street wine shops

Millennium? What Millennium? STREETPLONK 2000 is about bargain wines NOW!

Gluck covers them all: **Fullers, Majestic, Oddbins, Spar, Thresher (including Wine Rack and Bottoms Up), Unwins, Victoria Wine and Wine Cellar.** Malcolm Gluck's annual guide to the best-value wines available at our top high street wine shops is without equal.

* Completely rewritten every year

* The most up-to-date wine guide you can swallow

* 'Gluck's descriptive vocabulary is all his own, and some of his judgements turn convention on its head' *Time Out*

HODDER AND STOUGHTON PAPERBACKS

COMING SOON:

SUPERPLONK 2000

Gluck's annual guide to supermarket wine

Millennium? What Millennium? SUPERPLONK 2000 is about bargain wines NOW!

Gluck's beady palate takes in **Asda, Booths, Budgens, Co-op, Kwik Save, Marks & Spencer, Morrisons, Safeway, Sainsbury's, Somerfield, Tesco and Waitrose.** SUPERPLONK is an annual quest for the best bottles at the bonniest prices by Britain's best-loved wine writer.

* Completely rewritten every year

* The most up-to-date wine guide you can swallow

* 'Mr Gluck makes a charming and witty host' *Guardian*

HODDER AND STOUGHTON PAPERBACKS

COMING SOON:

THE SENSATIONAL LIQUID

Gluck's Guide to Wine Tasting

Britain's bestselling wine writer shows – with wit and without pretension – how to get the most pleasure from wine in his first fully illustrated hardback.

For too long, the world of wine tasting has been the preserve of a select few. Now Malcolm Gluck cuts through the pretension, and explains all the mysteries, from how to spot a corked bottle to what kind of glass to select. He shows how wine tasting involves each of the senses, and only when we have tuned all of these can we truly appreciate a wine. Innovatively written, illustrated and designed, THE SENSATIONAL LIQUID will be indispensable to all those who want to learn how to take their enjoyment of wine drinking to even greater heights.

HODDER AND STOUGHTON PAPERBACKS